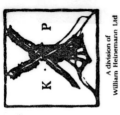

The Kingswood Press

10 Upper Grosvenor Street, London W1X 9PA
TELEPHONE 01 493 4141   TELEX 8954961   TELEGRAMS Sunlocks London W1

A division of
William Heinemann Ltd

THE REAL TRUTH ABOUT THE GOLF SWING

Theo Luxton

£9.95

Publication Date: 3rd February, 1986

A copy of your review would be appreciated

THE REAL TRUTH ABOUT
THE GOLF SWING
Theo Luxton

Illustrations copyright © 1985 by Phil Green

Text copyright © 1985 by Theo Luxton

Designed by Caroline Reeves

Published by The Kingswood Press, Kingswood, Tadworth, Surrey
An imprint of William Heinemann Ltd

Typeset by August Filmsetting, Haydock, St. Helens
Printed and bound by Garden City Press Ltd., Letchworth

0 434 98061 7

THE REAL TRUTH ABOUT
THE GOLF SWING
Theo Luxton

Illustrated by Phil Green

THE KINGSWOOD PRESS

CONTENTS

ACKNOWLEDGEMENTS

There were many times whilst I was working on this project, and during the writing of the book, when the whole thing became something of an obsession. Unearthing the truth, whatever the subject, usually involves a great deal of hard work. Unlike opinions, feelings and ideas, there is only one real truth. It may be simple, it may be complicated, but it often takes a lot of finding.

I shall always be grateful to my wife June who put up with a great deal of dedicated but often obsessive behaviour. Her quiet patience, and calm, feet-on-the-ground attitude helped me to arrive at my goal in one piece.

My thanks to Barry Bates, a golf professional, who took my doctrines to heart and combined with me to present several forums, thus spreading the ''gospel'' at least locally.

My thanks are due also to Walter Hooper and son Royston, whose busy light engineering and sheet metal fabrications factory constructed my two golf machines, without asking anything in return. These are the sort of people needed by inventors, particularly in Britain, if more use is to be made of their inventive and innovative talents.

1: Bobby Jones's swing, caught in a multiple-exposure photograph: 'I was hooked on this picture. I knew it held a secret.'

1: WHO IS THIS CRANK?

Like a lot of other people, I took up golf because I had become too old for football, my eye too slow for cricket and, for me, tennis was another name for strawberries and cream, all mush and very little bite. Golf was a game that had never been fully understood or conquered by the people who played it and who were fascinated by it. It was still a mystery and gave to me hours of enjoyment trying to fathom out how to hit the ball straight and then left me wondering how the Hogans, the Thomsons and the Lockes, stars of that day, kept the ball on the end of a piece of string. Being a natural ball player, golf intrigued me and, being an engineer, this sideways-on game had me wondering a little as to how the club put the ball into flight.

But in the early days, I was not too much bothered about the dynamics. I enjoyed the thrill of watching the ball drop on to a beautifully cared-for green and I took my pleasure from sinking a curly nine-foot putt which gave me the match against my old friend Harry, who then stood me a half pint of beer at the bar. And we talked about those shots which had given so much satisfaction – and about those that had not been so good. In those days I was an engineer playing an ancient game for pleasure and relaxation.

The year was 1967 and at that time I was working with the Central Electricity Generating Board in Bournville, Birmingham and playing my golf quite successfully off a handicap of 7 at Halesowen Golf Club. I suppose even then I was a bit of a golfing maniac and it was not surprising that a colleague in the drawing office gave me an American golf instruction book written by Dante and Elliot, a golf professional and a golf writer, who put together a quite useful book called *The Four Magic Moves to Winning Golf*. For me, however, it was the key which took me into a new world where the mysteries of golf no longer existed. It helped me see the light. It was a book after my own heart with its distinct flavour of a scientific approach.

This fascinated me, and more so, when I discovered that the authors had asked a professor at the Institute of Technology in Massachusetts to analyse the complete swing of a top class professional player frozen in a high-speed multi-flash photograph. The well-known picture of Bobby Jones is a fine example. I was hooked on this picture. I knew it held a secret. I was particularly intrigued by the fact that the wrists (the shirt cuffs in the photograph) appeared to slow down as the club approached impact with the ball at the bottom of the swing.

This was confirmed by the American scientist who gave a most interesting explanation that energy was being fed from the upper and rotating part of the body (the shoulders and arms) into the club head thus obeying the law, "conservation of angular momentum". The energy lost by the hands and arms caused them to slow down whilst the energy gained by the club head helped it to speed up. A very good analogy is that of the spinning ice skater who gathers momentum when he tucks his arms in and slows down when he pushes his arms outwards. In other words, energy is not lost, it is simply transferred.

A more simple and certainly a more complete way to look at it is to think in terms of centrifugal force which has two main components, one which is directly behind the club head speeding it into impact and one which acts directly outwards from the central pivot (the neck) through the club head trying to make it fly away from the body. It is this second component which causes the hands to slow down as impact is approached even though most golfers are trying hard to keep the hands moving as fast as possible through impact. It was the thought that the golf swing is amenable to scientific investigation that set me wondering about the possibilities of building a machine to demonstrate and prove things which up to that time had not been properly researched. For instance, just how important are the hands in a good swing and what is their true role?

For three months in the winter of 1967, I spent much of my spare time striving to make sense of that photograph, a captured series of arms going through a golf swing. I measured the length of the club in the picture and found a scale by basing my calculations on 43 inches, the average length of a driver. I measured my own arms and put a length on those in the photograph. I put the point of a compass into the neck, which is the major axis of the swing, and drew a circle to find that the path of the wrists was an oval one. Gradually, on a rough but surprisingly accurate mathematical basis, I built up a scientific picture and from it made my first elementary swing machine. It was a pendulum system, 18 inches high, made in hardboard. The shoulders and arms were represented by one lever (the upper one), the wrists were a simple hinge which connected the upper lever to the bottom lever (the club). Here we had a two-flail system. It was set up in a frame and to give a little more kick than just gravity I introduced a winder to put some power into the "shoulder action". All rather Heath Robinson but, nevertheless, it worked. It could hit, with some power, one of those plastic practise balls the length of my hallway at home.

This was success and it was back to the drawing board. I had proved to myself that I had found a formula, no matter how simple at this stage, that needed development. Slowly I put theory into practise and produced drawings for a full-scale swing machine. It is at this point that an inventor needs friends. Someone had to build it. I showed plans to a golfing pal, the chairman of an engineering firm specialising in sheet metal work and asked him for a

quotation to do the job. He took the plans away and the next thing I knew I was staring at the machine in the corner of a workshop in Oldbury, Birmingham.

There it was, a monster, a grotesque thing of iron and steel, standing six feet high and, as I found out later, weighing some 390lb, so heavy, in fact, that two people could not lift it. My friend was as enthusiastic as I was. He had done the work for love and he too was thrilled as we watched the 'thing' hit a real golf ball some 120 yards across a field with a remarkable degree of accuracy.

Now I was getting somewhere. I knew I had found a secret and wanted to know more about it. The machine needed more power. I tried heavy elastic bands on the wrist pivot to simulate the action of the right forearm and to put power in the 'wrists' early, though not too early, in the downswing. The energy for the all-important shoulder pivot was provided by a set of chest expander springs. I'll admit it was heavy, cumbersome and far from being complete in assimilating the true movements of the golfer. I could not stop: it was back to the drawing board again. Now I wanted to reproduce the true-to-life movement.

I always knew I would solve the problems with which I collided constantly during the development of the machines. There were, of course, disappointments and minor triumphs. In 1969 I demonstrated the 'iron monster' on Tomorrow's World, a television programme which gives encouragement to cranky inventors like myself and I guess I thought I had hit the big time. The publicity brought an immediate response from the golf trade. Accles and Pollocks, one of the world's leading manufacturers of golf club shafts, showed a big interest in the machine and sent a team along to study the possibility of using it as a test bed for their own research into the action and the work of a shaft. But I heard nothing more after the initial flutter of interest. Then Bob Haines, research manager of Inter-

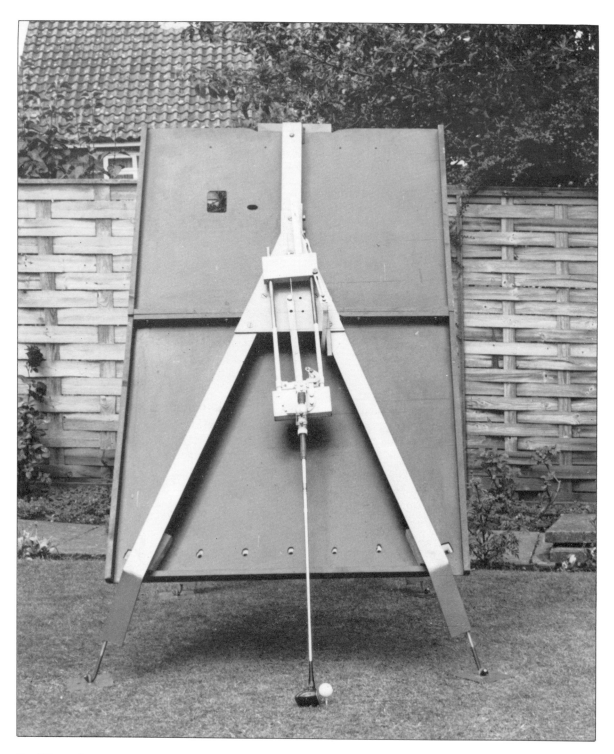

2: 'There it was, a monster, a grotesque thing of iron and steel, standing six feet high and, as I found out later, weighing some 390lb.'

3: 'Finally I had designed a cam system which made this second machine, the Luxton Mk II, the perfect demonstrator of the golf swing.'

national Sports Company, visited my home with a view to adapting the machine to test clubs and balls. In turn, I visited his research department at the Slazenger factory in Barnsley, Yorkshire, where he was using strain gauges on shafts to produce oscilloscope traces for analysis. These clearly showed that a maximum forward bend occurs in a shaft before impact thus proving quite conclusively that the shaft does not whip through the ball with its own flexing as most golfers, and even some manufacturers, have believed over the years. But, more of that later.

And then, in 1971, the iron monster was featured in the Alcan golf film, *Think of that whilst you're swinging*. For me this was success. My enthusiasm increased month by month as I realised I was on to something very important to the world of golf instruction. My theories and findings were constantly being confirmed by consultations and correspondence with such scientists as Bertie Daish, a leading ballistic expert and Dr Alistair Cochran, chairman of an investigating team of scientists (which included Bertie Daish) which produced the book *The Search for the Perfect Swing*. Another fascinating book by Dr David Williams, a Farnborough scientist called *The Science of the Golf Swing*, confirmed my ideas most emphatically. No one, at this point of time, had put all this information into a thorough-going teaching document and my project was directed into this area.

I puzzled my way through the complexities of the human frame going through all the 'gears' to put a golf ball into flight. By 1975 I had cracked three-quarters of the problem. I had ferretted out the seven pivot points which in my opinion, are the key factors in the swing movement and had incorporated them all in a half-size machine. But I wanted this machine to be perfect and I was driven to make it so by the desire to communicate with golfers in a vivid and realistic way because I felt they were getting a raw deal, not intentionally so, of course, from the teaching professionals.

The last problem was how to get the club shaft to rotate on its own axis through 180° so that the machine faithfully depicted the opening and closing of the club face through the backswing, downswing, and follow through. This took me another two years to solve. Again there were moments of despair, elation and despair but finally I had designed a cam system which made this second machine, the Luxton Mk II, the perfect demonstrator of the golf swing.

It had been a long time-consuming project, but never did I think of giving it up. It cost time and money but it was all worthwhile. I had found a secret and upon it built a golf theory. My machine, plus a 12-inch ruler and a flail (a broomstick cut in half and joined with a rubber hinge), are the three props that allow me to show how and why the swing is a two-flail system. In the 1970s I found a believer in my work; a professional golfer, Barry Bates from the Brandhall club in the West Midlands, and together we have spread this gospel of mine at small demonstrations in the area. And we have many followers who now share my secret and play better golf.

Now I want to tell the world all about it and that is the reason for this book.

2: THE TRUTH

Who is the most exciting golfer the world has ever known? There's no doubt about it. It's Sevvy Ballesteros, the man from Spain who makes golf look so easy, so natural. He has won all the titles, toured the world demonstrating his thrilling skills of mighty hitting, delicate iron play and uncanny accurate putting. A great professional, a man of fine character and truly modest in his successes. Here's a man who plays golf like no other and he must know what he puts into his swing to make it one smooth rhythmic powerful movement of human machinery. He produces shots which leave us all breathless. Surely he is able to explain and catalogue how it all works; which part of the body moves first as the swing is put into motion, what happens to the arms and hands, what happens to the club as it goes up and what path it takes as it comes down into the ball and what happens as the clubface smashes the ball into space.

But, here and now, I tell you he does not understand the true mechanics of the golf swing, let alone explain it. Ballesteros, like 99% of all the world's best golfers, past and present, does not know what really happens when he addresses the ball on the tee, takes the club back on the swing and then with infinite precision sends the ball 280 yards down the middle of the fairway. As ridiculous as it may seem Ballesteros cannot truly explain what he does or how he does it. Oh! he's tried all right; in books, in strip drawings and at clinics. But every time he gets so much of it wrong. And, he is not the only one. Jack Nicklaus and his coach, Jack Grout and our own great Henry Cotton do not understand or fully appreciate how the golf swing of champions comes together in a scientific sequence.

But, I know the full truth, will explain it to you in detail and make golf a much easier game to understand. I will explain what really happens when the ball flies away perfectly at the target and I will disclose and explain the real and only secret which will enable a player, professional or one of those many hundreds of thousands of individuals who take enjoyment and much frustration from the most intriguing game man ever invented, to improve his ability out of all recognition.

One of my favourite sayings is '*the truth is much deeper than you first imagine*' and some 17 years ago, as I have explained already, I began an intensive and orderly study of the game. Apart from other things, I was quite convinced that the teaching standards in Great Britain were, and still are, lower in golf than in most other sports. When you think about this it is not surprising. The overall swing, backswing, downswing and follow-through last about one second and a half. In fact, the business part of the swing, *i.e.* the downswing only, lasts for something like a quarter of a second during which time the clubhead accelerates from 0 to well over 100 mph. Once the club is on the way down the player himself can do nothing to alter or stop his swing unless he has already made up his mind to do so before reaching the top of the backswing. What all this means in simple language is that it is extremely difficult for even an expert player to fully understand the movement of all the bits and pieces. Even observing someone else is not easy and it is tempting to pretend you have seen something so as not to appear ignorant. It is therefore understandable that so many false ideas and misconceptions have been built up over the years. Very little teaching is built on solid fact.

Whilst I was working on those two machines I studied the action of players, both short and long handicaps. My first startling realisation was the extremely vital and important fact that all golfers are DOUBLE PENDULUMS. Put another way, all golf swings, are TWO-FLAIL systems. I will explain. Picture the pendulum in a grandfather clock shown in *Diagram 4*, and you will see a single pendulum. Now, if you cut in half the swinging rod in that clock and put in a second pivot or hinge at the break, you have created a double pendulum. By simply introducing a second "hinge", just as a golfer does when he picks up a club, you have altered the dynamics of the system dramatically because the lower lever will accelerate at a tremendous rate, as the bottom of the swing is approached, due to two major factors — centrifugal force and transfer of momentum.

All golf swings are two flail systems and the effect that this one all-important fact will have on teaching methods and doctrines over the coming years will be profound and far reaching. It is the most important factor to come to light since the game began. All other factors supplement, are an addition to, this major scientific fact, which must takes its place at the very centre of the jigsaw puzzle which when I have completed it forms the whole picture of golf teaching. I position the centre piece and place all the other pieces around it to complete this gigantic puzzle to form a clear picture in this book.

Soon after putting the 'iron monster' together I began corresponding with Bertie Daish, the ballistic expert, who was deeply involved with a scientific group study of the game promoted by The Golf Society of Great Britain and it was this research which produced the book *The Search for the Perfect Swing*. This work is dedicated to the memory of Sir Aynsley Bridgland whose imagination and enthusiasm made the investigation possible. The chairman of the team and co-author of the book, Alistair Cochran, kindly agreed to consult with me in order to see how my teaching theories would help him and fit in with the findings of his team of experts. An interesting exercise considering he had at one time played scratch golf as well

This is a long way from golf but it is a perfect illustration of a double pendulum or "two link flail system"

4

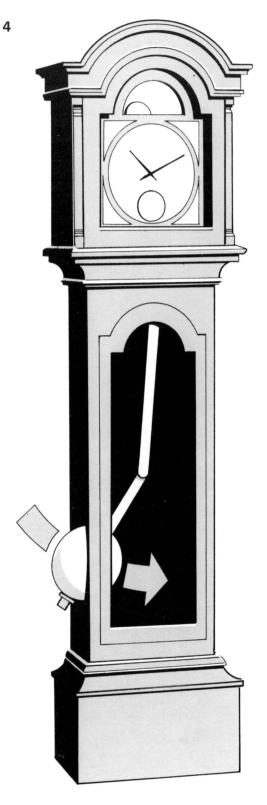

as being deeply involved with a project which is considered now to be the most comprehensive and exhaustive technical study of the game. Meetings and discussions with such authorative people strengthened my resolve to try and put right the balance on the teaching side of things. Being an enthusiast I was soon building my Mark II machine, this time one half full size with a pair of shoulders, two arms, wrists and a miniature golf club (*diagram 3*). This illustrated some very important aspects of the swing.

I gathered around me a small band of amateurs and professionals who had more than a passing interest in my new-found knowledge and ability. It gave me the greatest pleasure to be able to cure a vicious slice or an almighty hook and even turn a slight fade or draw into a consistent straight shot in the space of less than an hour. What was also very important, the pupil knew and understood the reasons why it had happened and why the cure had been made.

The saddest aspect of golf tuition is that it is difficult for golf professionals, who teach the game to the world, to accept this new scientific knowledge. The accepted instruction has been handed down, father to son so to speak, and the younger breed of teaching professionals are obviously steeped in these well-set ideas. This is one of the reasons why Britain, in particular, has fallen behind the world in so many different fields, other than sport. The Germans and Japanese are not so conservative or sensitive about the manner of gaining new knowledge; they are not adverse to stripping down other people's machinery to see what makes it tick. So I believe we should get off our backsides and actually do something about teaching golf. With this in mind, I present this book, *The Real Truth about the Golf Swing*, as a new and exciting concept of golf instruction.

I call this concept "teaching golf dynamically" which, in simple language, is instruction of movement and of the forces causing movement. One of the many secrets of my success in this method is to have my pupils swinging continuously, back and forward, back and forward, and then talking them into doing things and feeling what they are doing whilst they are actually swinging the club backwards and forwards. This is a very effective way of putting it across, much more convincing than the usual single, just once up and down, swing method. It is my experience that golfers find it very difficult to put any instruction into practise during a single swing and be expected to 'feel' what they have done in such a short space of time as one second and a half.

I describe the results of my methods as magical.

LUXTON'S GLOSSARY OF TERMS

DYNAMICS OF THE SWING
A study of the movements of the body and club during the swing, and of the forces (created by muscles and momentum) which cause these movements.

SWING PLANE
A plane best imagined as a pane of glass (with a hole for the head) sitting on the shoulders, its bottom edge (for an "on line" swing plane) resting at the ball position and in line with the target.

KINETIC ENERGY
Energy produced by motion i.e. anything that moves contains kinetic energy by virtue of its movement.

CENTRIFUGAL FORCE
Any body (such as a clubhead) moving in a circular or curved path is attempting to fly away from its centre and the force which is deemed to be trying to do this is called centrifugal force. This force is created by the kinetic energy of a body moving in a curved or circular path.

A SINGLE PENDULUM
As in a grandfather clock – a single lever with a pivot (hinge if you like) at its top end, and a weight at the bottom end.

A DOUBLE PENDULUM/A TWO-LINK FLAIL SYSTEM
Imagine the pendulum in the grandfather clock, now cut it in two and fit a hinge at the cut – you now have a double pendulum, but I prefer to call it a "two-link flail system".

LATE RELEASE
It means that, after the hands have left the clubhead behind during the first part of the downswing, the clubhead is allowed to begin its tremendous acceleration by a "late release" of clubhead kinetic energy, with the late uncocking action of the hands.

SWING PATH
Route of the clubhead "through the ball" at impact.

ON-LINE SWING
When the swingpath at impact is on line with the body aim. Therefore, if the body is aiming at the target the clubhead is also swinging on target. If the clubface is square at impact to its own swingline a perfectly straight on target shot is the result. Super, that's perfection!

IN-TO-OUT SWING
When the swingpath at impact is on a line which points to the right of where the body is aiming.

OUT-TO-IN SWING
When the swingpath at impact is on a line which points to the left of where the body is aiming.

SQUARE CLUBFACE
Points in the direction of the swingpath at impact.

CLOSED OR SHUT CLUBFACE
Points to the left of the swingpath at impact.

OPEN CLUBFACE
Points to the right of the swingpath at impact.

DRAWN SHOT
Curves slightly to the left.

HOOKED SHOT
Curves violently to the left.

FADED SHOT
Curves slightly to the right.

SLICED SHOT
Curves violently to the right.

PUSHED SHOT
Flies straight but to the right of the body aim.

PULLED SHOT
Flies straight but to the left of the body aim.

THROWING FROM THE TOP
When the hands at the very start of the downswing begin uncocking the wrists much too soon. One of the big problems for the average golfer.

3: MISCONCEPTIONS

This chapter must be thoroughly digested by all readers who have started to play the game and wish to improve on a permanent, no gimmick basis. Any one who has read golf instruction books or watched the game on television and listened to experts must be astounded by the variety of conflicting theories which are put across to the innocent. As I said earlier very few professionals have any real scientific knowledge. They have learnt their game from their mentors and then combined this grounding with their own experiences of playing, reading, studying and teaching. And, which ever way you look at it, a golf swing, good or bad, remains a technical mystery to the majority of professionals.

It is true that the Americans and Japanese are way ahead of the British in terms of knowledge of swing dynamics but they are not yet individually teaching the full truth. I could quote examples from American books where even basic facts as to what happens at impact when the clubhead meets the ball are completely wrong. As for the the British mentality, it is far too conservative to even want to search for the real truth. I prefer to unfold the whole truth of how the swing should be taught like a gigantic jigsaw puzzle having at its centre the most important and vital FACT of all – all golfers are two-flail systems. This is a simple and irrefutable fact of nature. But, firstly let me dismiss the untruths of the golf swing.

MISCONCEPTION No 1: The late hit

Many, probably most instructors, believe quite wrongly that the hands supply a good deal of the power, particularly in the later stages of the downswing. As most golfers know the hands in the professional downswing have moved to a position almost opposite the right leg whilst the club has reached a position approximately horizontal or nearly parallel with the ground, see *diagram 5*. This is known as the 'late hit' position and many theorists state that the professional then whips the club through to the ball with his strong hands. I know that most amateurs have tried to get into this 'late hit' position with often disastrous results such as pushing, slicing and difficulty in getting fairway wood shots off the ground. In an effort to overcome these problems teachers can be heard, day in and day out, 'You are not getting your hands through' and, 'You have not sufficient hand speed'. Both these statements are far from the truth and the more golfers try to hit with the hands the worse the problems become and the 'swinging' action of the true swing becomes more and more elusive.

5

The so-called "late hit" position

6: One source of the 'late hit' idea: pictures like this one of Arnold Palmer, showing a fictitious and exaggerated bend in the golf club shaft.

The real problem is that in trying to 'hit late' golfers grip much too tightly thus preventing the *full release* of clubhead kinetic energy (energy of motion). This gripping too tightly prevents the club from virtually catching up the left arm at impact. An additional and most disastrous effect of the clubhead being too far behind the hands at impact, particularly in a club player's swing is that the clubface is left open (more about that later) thus putting slice spin on the ball. Where did teachers get the 'late hit' idea? One of the main sources was the photographs which showed fictitious and exaggerated bends in the golf club shaft during the downswing into the ball together with the knowledge that the hands of the first-class player were far ahead of the clubhead as impact was approached. A host of these photographs similar to *diagram 6*, published in magazines and books, not only show the shaft bending viciously but also bending in a direction opposite to the actual truth. The villain in this piece is the focal plane shutter camera which can so easily tell a big fat lie. It is notorious for showing amazing distortions of high speed actions and this is an accepted fact in the photographic world.

The shaft in this position in the swing does not bend like this at all. In truth it bends slightly forward, slightly towards the ball, so that the clubhead is nearer the ball than the shaft which is entirely due to the effects of centrifugal force. This will be explained and illustrated in detail later but I had to include it here as part of a major misconception.

When analysing these photographs the teaching world thought that the hands, in the process of 'whipping the clubhead through', would apply tremendous leverage and therefore bend the clubshaft in this way. All fantasy because as I have just stated the shaft does not bend like this. Much damage to the player's ability has been caused by this theory. Most amateurs have tried to get into the late hit position at some time and sliced all over the place despite trying to get the hands 'through'.

The real truth is that there is no such thing as late hitting. Most of the clubhead speed is created by the club's own kinetic energy causing a tremendous acceleration provided the grip is light and gentle enough to allow it during the second half of the swing. This kinetic energy is given to the clubhead during the first part of the downswing by the hands pulling along the axis of the shaft without any uncocking action. There is no late hit in the last part of the classic downswing but there is a late *release* of clubhead energy.

MISCONCEPTION No 2: Hit hard with the hands

This adage is quite a favourite amongst some of the older pundits. Once again this carries with it the idea that there is a great deal of power in the hands. The idea was borne out of those wretched photographs I have just mentioned combined with the impression that the professional felt he was using his hands powerfully through impact. It is natural for anyone to believe that whatever their hands are feeling is actually happening at precisely that moment of time. When scientists investigated this factor they asked rational questions. 'How long does it take for the nerve ends in the fingers and hands to send their 'feel' message to the brain?' 'How far does the clubhead travel in this time?' The answer to the first question is 100th of a second and the answer to the second is approximately $1\frac{1}{2}$ feet as impact is approached. The conclusion is that the golfer feels the clubhead when it is $1\frac{1}{2}$ feet further on in the swing than he thinks and the lesson to be learned is that it is most unwise to formulate doctrines from 'feelings' without scientific investigation.

The real truth is that hitting hard with the hands does more harm than good because it gives free rein, psychologically speaking, to an already natural and strong desire which must be fought against. There are several examples showing that strong hands are not necessary for long hitting. Jack Nicklaus is one. There are also many cases showing that the shaft, and therefore the hands, are doing no work at impact. The scientists who stage-managed the 'search for the perfect swing' arranged for golfers to hit many shots with a driver which had a hinge in the hozel (the neck) just above the clubhead. High speed photographs, undistorted ones, showed that the hinge did not break or move during impact and demonstrated quite conclusively that the clubhead behaves as if it is in orbit (on its own so to speak) around the body.

One of the most important truths to arrive on the golfing scene in recent years is that the shaft of a golf club has little or no effect on the clubhead's behaviour at the moment of impact.

MISCONCEPTION No 3: It is impossible to hit too early with the hands and wrists provided you start the downswing with the legs working.

From a hands point of view, this doctrine is virtually the opposite to the 'late hit theory'. Now the thinking has swung the other way; first it was 'hit late', now it is 'hit early'. If you start the downswing with the legs (a correct doctrine) it is quite wrong to use the hands early in a leverage manner. This 'leverage concept' is the only way in which the average golfer will interpret the statement, 'it is impossible to use the hands too early'.

This simply means that the pupil will throw the clubhead much too early with the usual consequences:
a) less clubhead speed, b) out-to-in swing, c) gripping too hard, d) much less chance of achieving a square clubface at impact.

This teaching lacks an understanding of the swing dynamics. The truth is simple. The hands must not apply leverage for at least the first third of the downswing. Nicklaus increases, perhaps I should say continues, his wrist cocking action into the downswing. The actual distance is a further 33° after the downswing has begun. He is able to do this because his wrist cock angle at the top of the backswing is 90° with a 'high hands' position. Most professionals cock their wrists to a greater degree leaving an angle of less than 90° between the left arm and the clubshaft at the top of the backswing. I certainly do not advocate that the average golfer should attempt to copy Nicklaus, however, it is most important to at least retain the wrist-cock for the first part of the downswing. The way to achieve this is one of golf's important secrets.

MISCONCEPTION No 4: Hit it hard, learn to be accurate later.

This concept is more often directed at the younger player, but nevertheless, in my opinion, is a retrograde step simply because, once again, it gives freedom where control is needed i.e. control of the desire to hit. This emotion is called 'hit impulse'. There is no doubt in my mind that 99% of golfers would benefit tremendously by going right back to very gentle swinging, obtain a more sensitive feel and understanding of 'sweet' timing and from there build up more power gradually, always keeping solid contact and accuracy as top priority. By solid contact I mean that the ball must be contacted on the 'sweet spot' of the clubface (that's the spot which is in line with the centre of gravity of the clubhead), the clubface must be square to its own line of travel and obviously its own line of travel should be on line to the target. I wonder how many golfers have at some time hit a really 'sweet' shot with apparent ease without knowing why?

MISCONCEPTION No 5: Ways of starting the downswing

a) Pull on the club grip as if pulling a bell rope.
b) Slide the hips over, moving the weight on to the left side.
c) Slam down the left heel.
d) Drop the right shoulder on the inside.
e) Use your hands and arms freely.
f) A wide arc in the backswing will help your downswing.
g) The clubhead must be accelerated right from the commencement of the downswing.
h) Start the downswing with the legs.

There are more but these eight key sayings will suffice to show how different and far apart the ideas have got. The real well-timed downswing is a combination of movements all closely timed and smoothly carried through, starting from the feet and working upwards. The leg muscles must be followed by the back muscles closely and evenly, nothing vicious, to rotate the shoulders, which are the real hub of the swing, on a correct plane. The hands and the arms are quite heavy (for the average man 20lb) and are thrown out, away from the centre of the hub, by their own momentum (centrifugal force), a fact of nature not realised by most golfers and, as far as I know, not mentioned before in any other teaching book. Ninety nine per cent of golfers should not consciously hit with the hands and arms. This in turn will help the wrists to act as well-oiled hinges as they should do.

MISCONCEPTION No 6: 'Methods' of swinging

a) The square method
b) The square to square method
c) Swing the clubhead
d) The open to shut method
e) The shut to open method

'Methods' are a stereotyped way of teaching and therefore each method can only apply to a small minority. In any case each method is different to the others often in its own fundamental understanding of the swing.

For goodness sake let us all get together and standardise the basic teachings on a proper foundation and in the process improve the standard of play for everybody. John Jacobs, rated one of Britan's finest teachers, has been reported as saying that good golf teaching is a grave responsibility of the establishments. If this is so then it is also their grave responsibility to examine and use the scientific facts. Not push them under the carpet as has been done up to now.

Now for a change let's for a moment look at a doctrine which is based on sound logic evolving from a scientific fact. Powerful muscles of the body, those in the legs and back, produce their greatest efficiency and give their greatest power when working comparatively slowly. One teaching emerging from this fact is that a gentle start to the downswing using these vital muscles in their right gear gives immense advantages in several ways. Not the least of these is that it leads to better timing of the club (the lower lever) in relation to the shoulder/arm block (the upper lever), which will not only give good clubhead speed but also better control of the sweetspot and square contact.

This doctrine of 'start the downswing gently' and the scientific fact of 'powerful muscles are in their right gear when working comparatively slowly' are pieces of my gigantic jigsaw. And this picture will never change because it is the TRUTH. What does change is the physical and mental make-up of each pupil, therefore application of the truth will always change in some minor degree from pupil to pupil.

MISCONCEPTION No 7: Bunker shot techniques

Almost all teachers advise only one stance, an open one, and an out-to-in swing with an open clubface through the ball. I do not quarrel with the open stance but I most certainly do not agree with the out-to-in swing with an open clubface. How can anyone expect to be really accurate with a swing which aims left of the target and a clubface which aims right of the flag? Of course, it can be argued that Gary Player is the finest bunker player of all time, even though the years are passing him by, and he uses an out-to-in swing with an open clubface and so do all the other top players. But why make it difficult?

Try it my way and you'll find the shot to be much easier. Use an open stance (not too open), address the ball opposite the left heel, line up the shaft with the chin and if the sand is soft, grind the feet into it in order to get a slightly lower swing path. Keeping the clubface *square to target both at address and at impact swing the club on line to the target entering the sand between one and two inches before reaching the ball*. I can guarantee better bunker results with this method. There will be plenty of height and backspin with a great deal of accuracy. This is the true way to play a bunker shot and I know it to be so.

MISCONCEPTION No 8: Golf is a simple game

Many teachers claim that golf is a simple game and then unwittingly they make the game more and more complicated as they proceed with their 'teachings'. Many of the great ball players of this world having taken up golf late in life pronounce it as the most difficult game of all. One of the main reasons for this is the low standard of instruction. And it must not be forgotten that golf is a still ball game in which a complicated series of body movements have to be programmed in to the mind and then carried out from a standing start in something like one and a half seconds. And another reason it is difficult is that it takes a greater amount of concentration to curb the 'hit impulse' in golf than in other games.

MISCONCEPTION No 9: Paralysis through analysis

This statement has been made by many pundits who believe that the swing should never be broken down into its separate parts because this clutters the mind with detail and brings about confusion and then paralysis. I am certain that the vast majority of golfers need to have detail and the truth is that paralysis, more often than not, arrives through incorrect analysis.

Teachers make the big mistake of attempting to introduce the swing as a single element to adult pupils. This method of instructing presupposes that we are all potentially natural golfers and this assumes that golf is a natural game with the swing therefore being a natural action. This is certainly not the case. Very few of us can expect our relatively untrained muscles to execute the combined twisting and rotating action of the swing with any real efficiency from the word go. In any case, understanding the swing as a whole can be achieved only by firstly understanding each part of it. The pupil must know what he is trying to do and how the elements of the swing fall into their correct order. Blundering from one error to another without any clear objective in sight will set up paralysis or at the very least total frustration.

SUMMARY

Golf is not and cannot be an easy game. If it was it would hardly be worthwhile taking the challenge.

Golf tuition has been confused by mystique because until recent years little concrete evidence has been available as to what really happens during good and bad swings. The swing is over so quickly that precise details of the movement escape the eye of even the most skilled observer. To avoid appearing to be ignorant, experts often claim to see more than is actually possible and straight away a doctrine is born which is perpetuated in countless books and magazines and endless conversations between golfers.

My first aim is to kill off all the important and destructive misconceptions and then I will show how the swing really works. After this will come my easy-to-understand simplified doctrines based on the TRUTH. My first line of thought begins in a seemingly complicated way in order to unravel the mumbo jumbo and then gradually the thinking becomes more simple and clearer as the jigsaw grows.

Provided my swing practices and other routines are worked through with a degree of diligence, magical improvement can be achieved. Work with the TRUTH and I guarantee you will experience a little MAGIC.

4: THE SECRET AND THE TRUTH

One of man's earliest inventions was the flail for threshing corn and it consisted of two sticks joined together with a piece of leather. The first stick was raised above the head, and the second stick hung downwards behind the first one, the leather joint being bent almost double. The stick was then swung downwards with an easy, graceful action. With the leather thong acting as a free pivot, the second stick whipped round and crashed to the ground at amazing speed and under the influence of its own kinetic energy. Now, here is the interesting factor – the whole action needed only a minimum expenditure of energy and that is exactly why the device came into use for its high degree of efficiency. Corn threshing went on throughout the long summer days and any device which conserved energy, but at the same time produced maximum beating speed, was invaluable.

Now think of the golf swing. In this threshing flail analogy the leather thong represents the wrists of the golfer, but the leather is not capable of applying a leverage to the second stick, yet the stick comes through at high speed. That must mean something and I will now give you a full explanation of the two-link flail system and the dynamics of the golf swing, stage by stage. Your understanding of these most important scientific facts will then be built up slowly and surely.

To go immediately to the heart of the matter, the ruler test is the easiest way to understand the two-flail system. Stand up, tuck your right elbow into your side and keep it there for this part of the test, holding the end of a 12" ruler (with a hole drilled as in the diagram) between your finger and thumb. Now swing the forearm forwards and backwards as shown in *diagram 7*. The forwards and backwards swinging

must be done continuously and be performed with a smooth rhythmical action. With a little practice you will soon find the right speed and acceleration to use in order to bring the ruler through the bottom position at a good pace, with a feeling that you have timed the swing of the forearm correctly. The pinching action of the thumb and first finger should only be sufficient to prevent the ruler from flying out of your hand.

If you grip the ruler too hard it has difficulty in moving through to the impact position and this is exactly what tends to happen when you grip the club too tightly in a proper golf swing. You should extend the above to include the wrist flexing (cocking) as also shown in *diagram 7* in the insert, but please bear in mind that the correct wrist movement in the actual golf swing is slightly different as fully described in a moment, and also later in the book, where you will see that the right hand climbs over the left as the clubface rotates through about 90° after impact and into the follow through.

This test is a good example of a two-link flail system and so closely related to the threshing flail. The golf swing is exactly this, a fact often repeated in this book in different contexts as a constant reminder of the most important discovery since the game began. All golfers from the beginner to the top tournament professional can easily improve their game from studying this fact, and by understanding how the body dynamics, that is to say the power and movement of the body, fits into this system.

Relating the ruler test in terms of a golf swing, the top pivot (the elbow) represents the golfer's shoulder pivot (the neck), the second

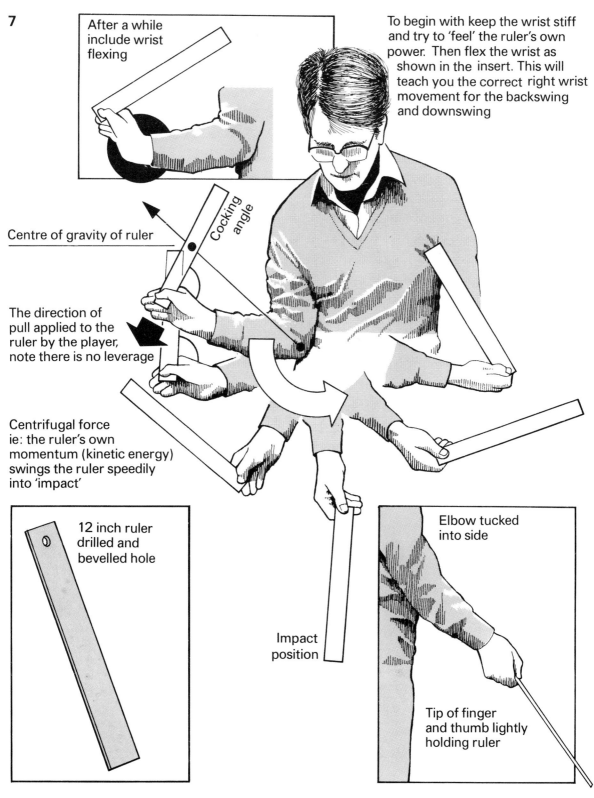

After a while include wrist flexing

To begin with keep the wrist stiff and try to 'feel' the ruler's own power. Then flex the wrist as shown in the insert. This will teach you the correct right wrist movement for the backswing and downswing

Centre of gravity of ruler

Cocking angle

The direction of pull applied to the ruler by the player, note there is no leverage

Centrifugal force ie: the ruler's own momentum (kinetic energy) swings the ruler speedily into 'impact'

12 inch ruler drilled and bevelled hole

Impact position

Elbow tucked into side

Tip of finger and thumb lightly holding ruler

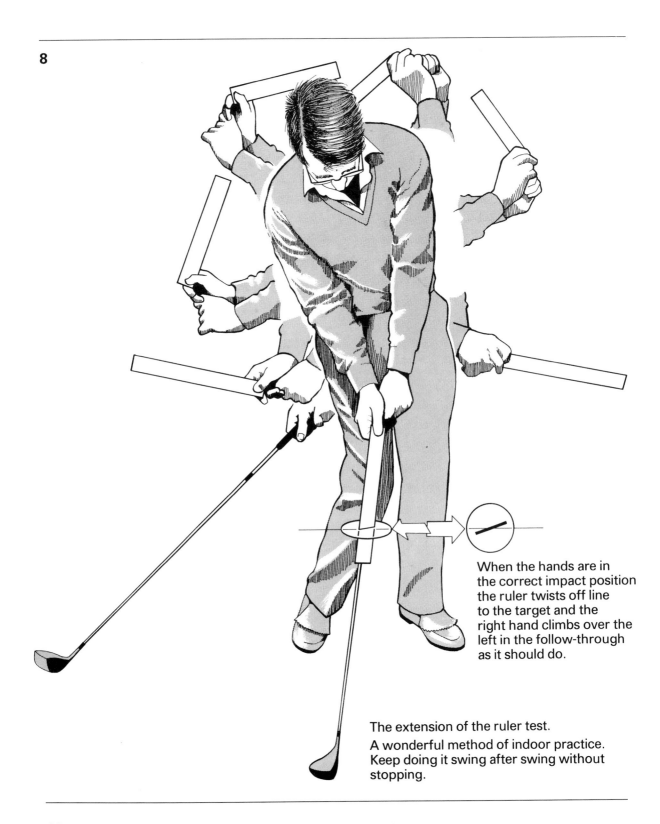

When the hands are in
the correct impact position
the ruler twists off line
to the target and the
right hand climbs over the
left in the follow-through
as it should do.

The extension of the ruler test.

A wonderful method of indoor practice.
Keep doing it swing after swing without
stopping.

pivot (the finger and thumb) represents the golfer's wrists pivot. The forearm represents the player's shoulder/arm block, and the ruler represents the golf club itself.

Now the simple ruler test can be extended because having discovered that the ruler really does have or contain kinetic energy you can go to another stage, see *diagram 8*. I want you to perform a full backswing, downswing, and follow through. Start, fairly gently, and introduce the combined pivoting and sliding motion of the hips. In other words, practise the body movements of legs rocking forwards and inwards so that the shoulders are rotating on plane about a reasonably stationary spine. *Diagram 8* depicts the ruler test "full swing" exercise whereby you have to imagine a club as you swing the ruler. This is important – the right elbow should lead the hands in to the impact at which position the forearms and hands will "overtake" through the address position. The right elbow should also brush across the front of the right side.

When you perform this exercise you will notice that the right elbow leaves your side just a little, and you should not attempt to keep it tucked in during the last stage of the backswing. It must return to the right side early in the downswing and then it should brush across the front of the right side as stated above. The ruler is entirely accelerated by its own kinetic energy. You must fully believe this TRUTH, the most vital fact associated with all golf swings.

A word of warning be careful the ruler does not fly out of your hand. The hands must begin to rotate the ruler in an anticlockwise direction just before impact, and after impact the right must climb over the left. This is necessary to ensure a square clubface at impact but you must *not* apply leverage to the imaginary club. Try to feel as though, during this full swing indoor practise, your hands are being uncocked by the weight (power) of the "clubhead", and the hands are freewheeling

through impact in response to clubhead power. A wonderful feeling to achieve because it obeys the two flail laws of dynamics. I can with absolute confidence assure you that, provided you get the movements reasonably correct,this indoor practise is quite wonderful but do it smoothly with beautiful and controlled relaxation.

So that you can feel the effect of clubhead kinetic energy with an actual club, I suggest that you swing one (with your left hand only) gently backwards and forwards without stopping, gradually increasing the length of the swing arc. Get the feel of the wrist operating smoothly as though it is a well oiled hinge. After doing this for a minute or so, put your right hand on the club so that you have a proper grip. Again swing the club gently backwards and forwards, rotating your shoulders about a spine which does not sway. You will now be aware of a greater control of the club and feel that there is no need to lever the club with the hands. In other words you should feel the clubhead doing a lot of work, just like the ruler which swung through quite happily not needing any leverage or torque at the pivot point. In fact, in your swing that pivot point is at your left wrist (where your watch is), and the energy built into the clubhead by "the pulling along of the shaft" during the first part of the downswing will uncock your wrists without any assistance from the hands at an amazing rate of knots, again, just like the ruler. As before, start gently with a small swing arc and gradually build up to a full or nearly full swing, trying to feel the clubhead as a weight at the end of a length of string.

Great emphasis is given to the free swinging action because I have found that it is one of the more difficult aspects of the game for the average player to grasp. Nevertheless, my properly designed practice tests are bound to help tremendously. Now try the right hand only, repeating the action, and with same objective of feeling the swinging action of the clubhead without hitting with the hand.

You are now experiencing the most important thing in golf: the feel of a swinging clubhead. It is the real secret and truth.

The full downswing is shown in simple diagram form in *diagram 9* and for this first step of the explanation I assume that at the wrist pivot there is no power at all. There are two distinct stages in the analysis of the downswing. The first stage is from the top of the backswing (*position A*), to the wrist cock release position (*position B*). The second stage is from *position B* to *position C* (the impact position). The two levers are the shoulders/arm block and the club.

The shoulder/arm block is represented in *diagram 9* by the shaded triangles. This triangle is pivoting about the shoulder pivot (the top of the spine or neck), and the club is pivoting about the wrist pivot which is actually the left wrist (right-handed golfer). As I have said, we are assuming that there is no power or leverage being applied at the wrist pivot.

In the first stage of the downswing the triangle rotates about the shoulder pivot with the wrist cock angle remaining constant. As the end of the first stage is reached, the energy which the clubhead now has, begins to throw out or rotate the second lever (the club) around the wrist pivot in the form of centrifugal force. This accelerates the clubhead into the impact position with considerable velocity even though there is no assisting leverage at the wrist pivot.

A side effect is that the rotational action of the lower lever reacts on the upper lever by slowing it down as impact position is approached.

This in turn helps to increase the momentum of the lower lever, and is a good example of the law "the conservation of angular momentum". I have not shown this in the diagram because the golfer must not try consciously to slow his arms down. He must, in fact, try to keep his shoulders and arms rotating through

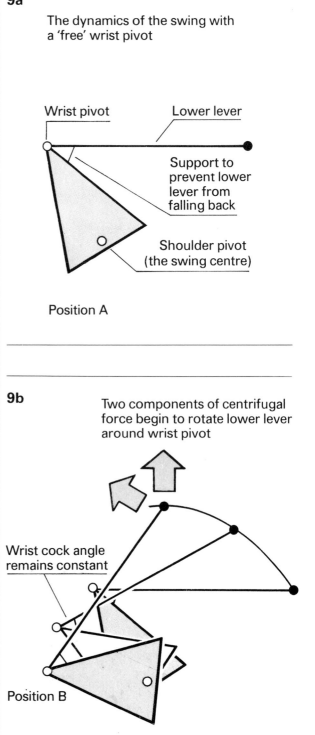

9a

The dynamics of the swing with a 'free' wrist pivot

Wrist pivot   Lower lever

Support to prevent lower lever from falling back

Shoulder pivot (the swing centre)

Position A

9b

Two components of centrifugal force begin to rotate lower lever around wrist pivot

Wrist cock angle remains constant

Position B

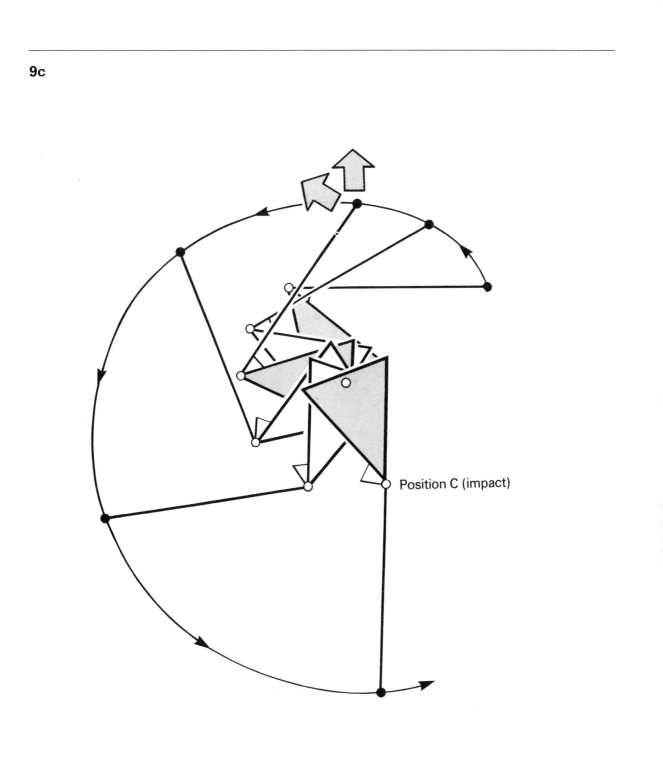

Position C (impact)

10

These four diagrams are views from above the golfer
and at right angles to the swing plane

POSITION A

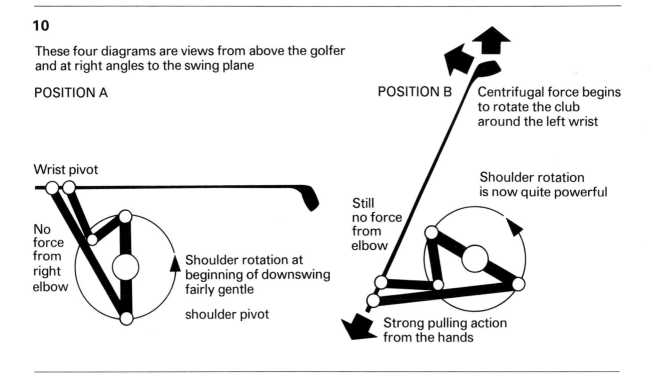

POSITION B

Centrifugal force begins
to rotate the club
around the left wrist

Wrist pivot

Shoulder rotation
is now quite powerful

No
force
from
right
elbow

Still
no force
from
elbow

Shoulder rotation at
beginning of downswing
fairly gentle

shoulder pivot

Strong pulling action
from the hands

impact in a smooth manner, even though
scientific analysis shows his "upper lever"
slowing down in the later stages of the
downswing.

This takes me now to the next step of the
explanation of swing dynamics. The true full
dynamic diagram of the classic downswing is
shown in *diagram 10*. It demonstrates how the
right hand and arm does apply a certain
amount of power to the wrist pivot. It is the
right elbow, in actual fact, that supplies most
of this power simply because it has to bend
during the backswing to allow the left arm to
move across the chest and it then straightens
during the latter part of the downswing to
allow the left arm to return to its address
position. To be accurate, the left arm returns to
beyond its address position, but at this stage
that is not important. The difference between
diagrams 9 and *10* is the addition of right
elbow power and this means that the wrist
release position (*position B* in *diagram 10*)

has to occur a little later in the downswing
than it does in *diagram 9* if maximum clubhead
speed is to be achieved with the minimum
amount of energy input. The timing of this
application of right elbow power, whilst it is
small in comparison to the major power input
(the legs and body muscles), is one of the
most difficult things to learn.

This is the full explanation of the true dynamics of the classic golf downswing in two
diagrams with *diagram 10* being the final
picture and looking very much like a golfer's
shoulders and arms in "stick" form. I have not
shown body and legs for a very important
reason. It is an excellent idea for you to think in
terms of rotating the "hub of the swing", the
shoulder pivot, to make sure of full use of the
large muscles of the legs and back. So the hub
has been shown in *diagram 10* as the centre of
action.

At this point I want to say more about the late

POSITION C
SOON AFTER POSITION B

POSITION D

Kinetic energy of clubhead now quite powerful

Shoulder rotation now powerful

Right elbow now assisting centrifugal force, but not overpowering it

Strong pull

Shoulder rotation still powerful

Right elbow force almost expended

Clubhead speed at maximum yet the golfer 'feels' as if it is freewheeling hit which incorporates a belief, still held by an amazing number of golfers, that if you delay the wrist uncocking action until you have reached hip height the hands will whip the clubhead at the ball. Most of these players will tell you that the hands are the source of a great deal of power and, as a result, some will advise hand strengthening exercises such as squeezing a squash ball. I want to put the late hit theory into proper perspective. A typical late hit position in the middle of the so-called hitting area is shown in Chapter 3. As I said earlier these are pictures taken by focal plane shutter cameras and show an abnormal backward bend in the shaft and a tremendous number of teachers concluded from this bend that the hands must be putting a lot of leverage on the shaft. This only shows that proper scientific study must be carried out to pry out the truth.

The truth of what happens to the shaft as it approaches impact is shown in *diagram 11*. It is bending slightly forwards and at the same time bowing outwards. This is entirely due to centrifugal force acting through the centre of gravity of the clubhead. This centre of gravity is, on all normal woods, both behind and outside the shaft. If you place a wood club on a table with the clubhead overhanging the edge, the clubhead will hang below the shaft and the face will tilt upwards at an angle of approx. 15° to the vertical. This angle will vary a little from one make of club to another. Centrifugal force in a classic swing used by Britain's Nick Faldo is at its maximum at the impact position, simply because the clubhead is travelling at its fastest speed and CF is a function of clubhead weight and speed. Therefore, the bending forwards and bowing outwards of the shaft is at its maximum just before impact. Final proof of the forward bend (to its maximum) of the shaft is shown in *diagram 12*.

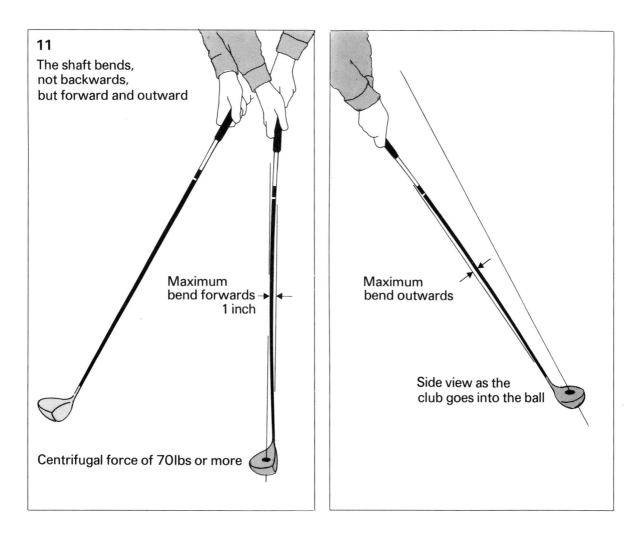

11

The shaft bends,
not backwards,
but forward and outward

Maximum
bend forwards →←
1 inch

Centrifugal force of 70lbs or more

Maximum
bend outwards

Side view as the
club goes into the ball

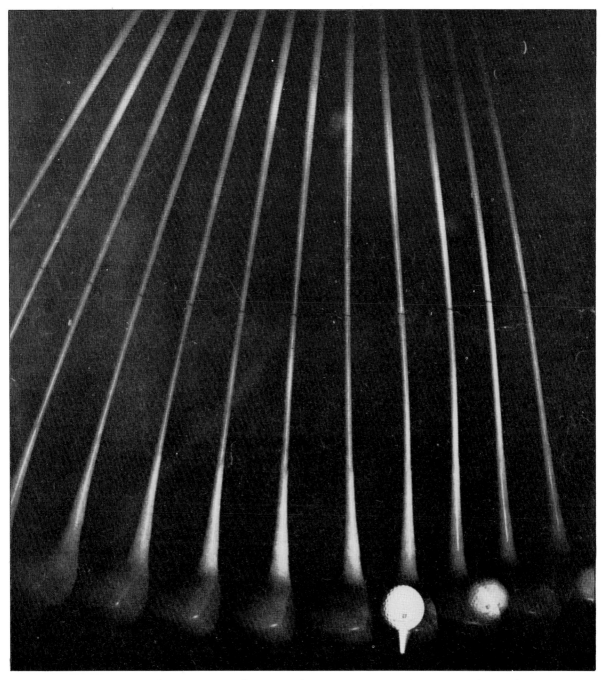

12: Photographic proof that the shaft bends forward was provided by this strobe sequence photo, made with each flash at one-millionth (1/1,000,000) sec, taken by Edgerton, Germeshausen and Grier, Inc., Boston, Massachusetts, U.S.A.

This is what happens to the shaft, but what about the clubhead? Centrifugal force, acting through the offset centre of gravity of the clubhead, "winds" it up. It closes the face a little and also slightly increases the loft. The increase in loft is, in fact, nullified by the closing effect. My golf machine shows this closing-up effect on the clubface quite clearly. it will only hit straight shots with a wood if the clubface is aligned at address in a slightly open position. This really means that every wood has a built-in draw characteristic, due entirely to the position of the centre of gravity of the clubhead being behind the shaft.

5: THE GRIP

Perhaps for some of you the scientific nature and content of the last chapter was hard going and you felt that you were a long way from golf. But you have been told for the first time the real secret of the game and now I am going to turn the jargon into a golf shot and your game is about to improve out of sight. This is going to be a new experience, a golf lesson as you have never had before.

To begin with I place far less importance on the grip than most teachers do. Whilst it is important you realise that the way you hold the club can affect the presentation of the clubface to the ball, it is vitally important to appreciate that the hands and wrists are not, I repeat, are not the primary source of power. But I am going to get your grip as it should be on the club.

Please stand up, and keep your arms hanging loosely at your sides. You will note that their natural position is when the palms face inwards and to make them face any other direction necessitates using arm muscle power. Now raise your arms forwards and keep the palms facing inwards. Bring the hands together palms touching so that the karate edge of the hands is a few inches (say 8 or 9 inches) away from the front of your body as shown in *diagram 13a*. From this position slide the right hand away from the body so that its little finger is opposite the first finger of the left hand as in *diagram 13b* – the basic position for the overlapping grip (most popular among professionals and amateurs).

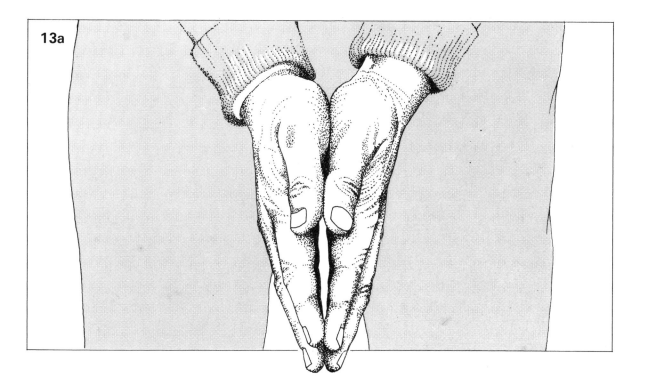

13a

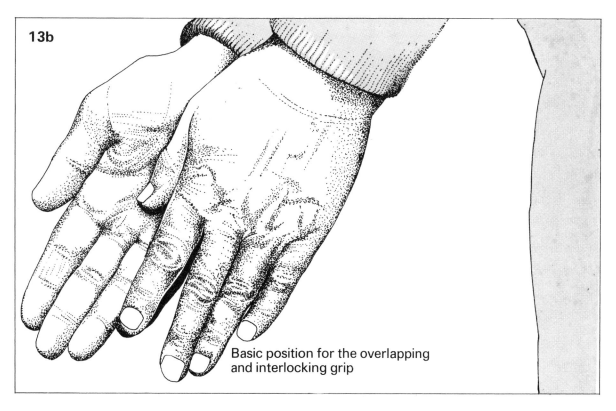

13b

Basic position for the overlapping and interlocking grip

43

The next step is to place a club so that the sole of the clubhead is flat on the ground, see *diagram 14*, and the grip is between the palms of the hands as shown in *diagram 15*. The face of the club and the bottom edge of the face (irons) must of course face the target, in other words be square to the line to target. Just a few beginners have the idea that it is the top edge of the clubface which should be square. They have not realised that the top edge of irons is angled to the bottom edge. So I repeat – keep the bottom edge square to target and the clubface will be square to the target. Ensure that the top of the club shaft (the handle) is below the heel of the left hand. In other words, hold it in the same way as you would hold a hammer, but not tightly.

14   Sole of club flat on ground

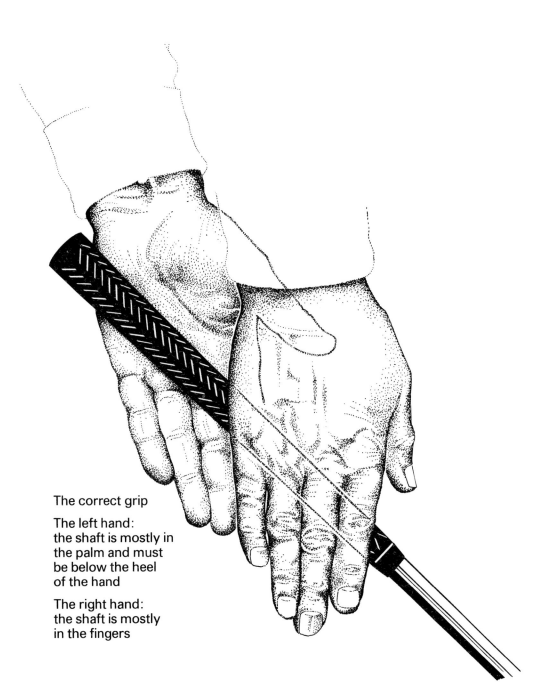

15

The correct grip

The left hand:
the shaft is mostly in
the palm and must
be below the heel
of the hand

The right hand:
the shaft is mostly
in the fingers

Now close the fingers and thumbs around the grip (*diagram 16*), making sure that the little finger of the right hand overlaps the first finger of the left hand. Better still – let the little finger of the right hand slip into the groove between the first and second finger of the left hand. The thumb of the left hand should be diagonally positioned across the grip and fit snugly into the palm of the right hand. It should not be placed on the top of the grip. The thumb of the right hand should be running diagonally across the left of the grip, and the first finger should be extended down the grip leaving a space between it and the second finger. The club must not be held in a vice-like grip, it must be held with a light touch and the holding should be done by the last *three* fingers of both hands. This completes the overlapping grip, the most popular amongst all golfers.

Having closed the hands as in *diagram 16* the Vs formed by the first finger and thumb of both hands should point in an imaginary line to each side of the chin. The clubshaft should be lined together with the 'V' of the left hand to just left of the chin. *Diagram 17* shows the hand and clubshaft alignment. Remember this is the basic alignment and will be subject to slight adjustment when you have become accustomed to swinging (I stress this word) the club.

The interlocking grip as shown in *diagram 18* is often used by golfers with small hands. The little finger of the right hand is interlocked with the first finger of the left and in so doing is more in contact with the grip. This gives a feeling of greater control once the peculiar interlocking feeling is overcome. It also means that the last three fingers of the right hand are more inclined to hold the club than the fore-finger which should in any case be spread down the grip leaving a space between it and the second finger.

16

The overlapping or Harry Vardon grip used by the majority of players

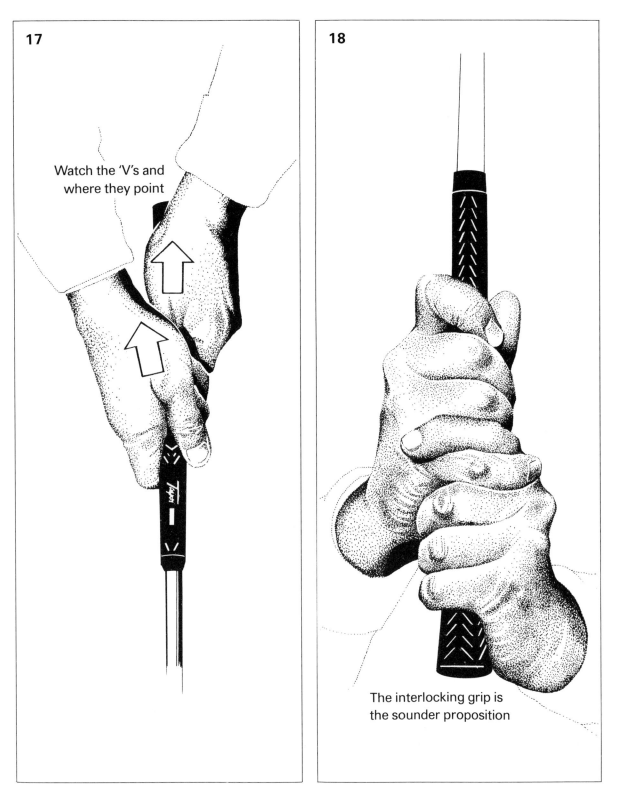

17

Watch the 'V's and where they point

18

The interlocking grip is the sounder proposition

In my opinion, the interlocking grip is a sounder proposition than the overlapping type because:

1. It enhances the essential concept of "grip with the last three fingers of both hands".
2. It does this because it automatically separates the first and second fingers of the left hand and in so doing it prevents the forefinger of this hand from wrapping closely round the grip and in fact gripping the club.
3. As already stated it enables the little finger of the right hand to partly wrap around and hold the club.

Many golfers do, however, find that interlocking the fingers feels uncomfortable and immediately shy away from this method. I suggest that they give it time before finally accepting the more common overlapping grip.

I do not recommend the two-handed grip. The two hands are basically separate and therefore the wrists are further apart than in the other two grips I have described. It must be understood that the wrists and hands are only capable of applying a small proportion of the total power. Their main function is first and foremost to transmit the power of the body to the club without interfering with the clubhead's own kinetic energy. It is not hand leverage that brings the clubhead to the ball with such impact speed, it is the proper use of the clubhead's own momentum (kinetic energy). A one-armed golfer in Scotland has exceeded 280 yards in a long driving contest, and there is no doubt that he knew how to develop tremendous clubhead speed without hitting with the hand.

Once again – ALWAYS GRIP LIGHTLY. Many teachers, Henry Cotton being foremost among them, advise a firm grip because they mistakenly believe that the clubshaft will twist in the hands, even with sweetspot contact. Try this test in order to convince yourself once and for all that this is a completely wrong idea: hold a club at the top of the handle with the finger and thumb of the right hand (or left if you are left-handed), and let it hang vertically. Now get a friend to tap the clubface in three different positions i.e. towards the toe, on the centre (the sweetspot) and towards the heel, with the edge of a 10p coin. Note which way the clubhead *wants* to turn, with the finger and thumb acting as feelers or sensors. When tapped towards the toe the clubface will turn outwards (open); when tapped towards the heel it will turn inwards (close); and when tapped on the sweetspot, which will take a few taps to find, the clubface will move *back without turning* (stay square). **THINK ABOUT THAT FOR A FEW MINUTES!**

You must understand this important scientific fact about impact. When the clubhead meets the ball on the sweetspot there is absolutely no twisting movement on the shaft, and, therefore, gripping firmly serves no useful purpose. Gripping firmly, however, does have an appallingly damaging effect on the swing as I have already demonstrated several times. When the ball contacts the clubface towards its toe then the clubshaft will be slightly twisted clockwise so that the clubface opens. The reverse happens when the ball contacts the clubface towards its heel, in this case the clubface closes. In both cases the "grip firmly" brigade are wasting their time and effort because nothing whatsoever can prevent this opening or closing effect on the clubface.

IMPORTANT POINTS TO REMEMBER ABOUT THE GRIP

1 Grip lightly, not tightly, and carry out these two tests to prove to yourself why this statement is so important.

   a) Hold the club straight out in front of you so that the shaft is roughly horizontal at about waist height. Get someone to pull the club directly away from you while you vary the strength of your grip. You will be surprised how lightly you can hold the club before it slips through your fingers.

   b) Hold the club as above and very tightly and ask your friend to move the clubhead from side to side. Now grip more lightly and note that it is easier for your friend to move the club. Now hold it progressively lighter and your friend will confirm that it becomes progressively easier to move the club thus proving that a tight grip inhibits the swinging action of the clubhead. In scientific language a light easy grip allows the clubhead's own kinetic energy to work more efficiently in the second part of the downswing.

2 Palms facing together or inwards is without doubt the best hand position for promoting wrist flexibility through impact. Persevere with this if it is a new position for you, particularly the left hand. Any experimentation should only be done after getting used to swinging the club with the basic position, and, in any case, should only consist of adjusting the right hand by rotating it slightly clockwise or anticlockwise, carefully, noting the change in ball flight. Turning this hand clockwise say $\frac{1}{4}''$ to $\frac{1}{2}''$ should either straighten a fade or put draw on a previous straight shot. A fade is a slight curve to the right, and a draw is a slight curve to the left (for the right handed golfer). Most professional teachers call this clockwise movement of the hand a strengthening of the grip. Moving the hand anticlockwise (weakening it)

should result in straightening a draw or putting a fade on a previous straight shot. These resulting changes in ball flights are more likely to happen after first learning to swing properly, with wrists that move like well-oiled hinges. I call them fluid wrists.

6: THE STANCE AND THE ADDRESS

I have taken you through the dynamics of the swing revealing the full truth of what happens in a way that I am sure is entirely unique. Now I will help you to use this two-flail system to acquire the skills which will have you playing this game of golf as you have never played it before. But, firstly, a warning note, and an important one at that. To remodel your game will not be easy because old habits die hard. Long term improvement will only come with a deal of patience, dedication and hard work. Throughout it all, I ask you to remember the ruler test which you carried out a short time ago while I was explaining my theory. That ruler is the key to your new game. It will be the reminder of the TRUTH. Now I will help you to put your swing and game together through its major component parts.

The stance and the address of the ball is the foundation from which the swing operates. The feet, for example, are vitally important because they set up the way the body is aimed at the target. They are the main base for the whole system and must be positioned so that the swing can operate smoothly and efficiently and in the right direction. To clarify this further if you turn the steering wheel of a car to the left this will turn the front wheels to the left and the car will move in that direction. If, however, you hold the steering wheel steady to go straight ahead that is where the car will travel. By examining *diagram 19* you can see that the wheel or "plane" of the swing, although tilted over to the left, is aiming at the target as are the feet (a line across the toes goes through the target). These feet are in

19a

The hub of the swing

The swing has foundations in stance and address

Think of wristwatch moving on a wheel aimed at target

19b

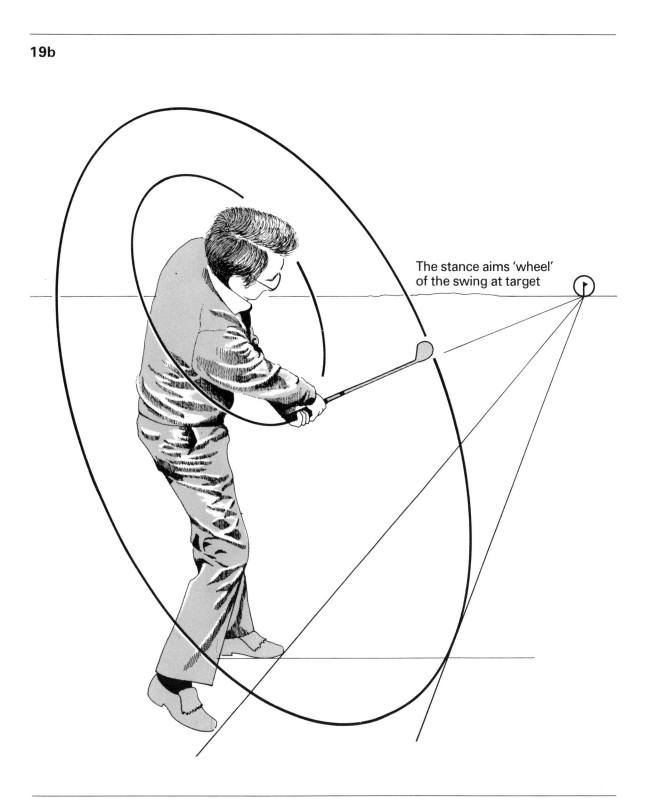

The stance aims 'wheel' of the swing at target

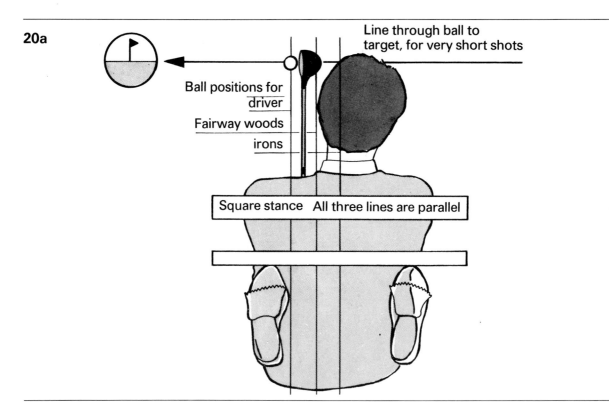

a SQUARE stance position, and for further clarification look at *diagram 20a*, a bird's eye view of the golfer in a square stance, and take particular notice of the shoulders also in a square stance position. Everything is in fact aimed at the target as it surely should be. I ask you to take notice of the shoulder alignment because it is quite easy to allow the right shoulder to set up an open shoulder position. This comes about with a slight forward movement due to the right hand being below and further forward than the left. Many golfers allow this to happen without realising it, and the cure is: tuck your right elbow back a little into your right front side to ensure "on line" shoulders.

So much for the body alignment, now for the ball position. Again refer to *diagram 20a* which shows three positions only, the left position is for a driver from a teed-up ball, the ·middle position is for fairway woods, and the

centre of the stance position is for all iron clubs except the sand wedge from a bunker. I do not agree with progressively moving the ball for each club in the bag because it is a complicated concept. Three positions are all that is necessary, and you need to understand that the following three angles of attack are associated with these ball positions: 1) where the driver or other wood clubs should ideally contact the ball slightly on the upswing with the ball being mounted on a tee 2) where the fairway woods sweep the ball off the ground and 3) where all irons contact the ball first before hitting the ground on a ball/turf concept, impacting the ball on a downswing path *before* the bottom of the swing. This has the effect of squeezing the ball to some degree into the ground, and in reasonable conditions this creates *maximum* backspin, very desirable for iron play. It helps to keep the shot on line whilst in flight and also for "pulling" the ball up short when landing on the greens, giving more control of the shot.

20b

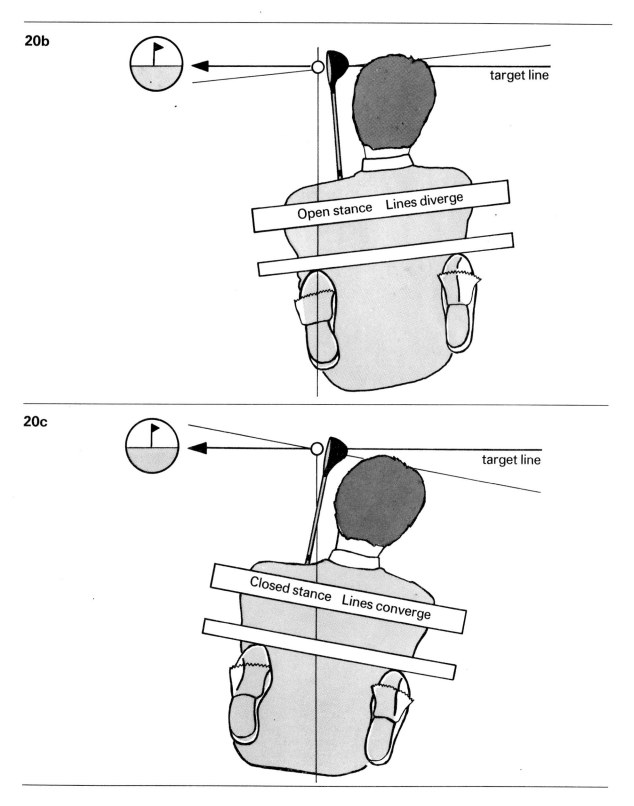

target line

Open stance   Lines diverge

20c

target line

Closed stance   Lines converge

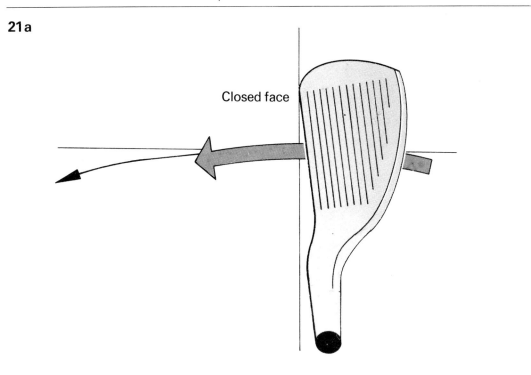

Closed face

The next component to get right is the club-head itself. Most instructors teach their pupils to place the clubhead behind the ball, squaring it to target, before doing anything else such as placing the feet. I do not agree with this method because simple geometry will tell you that the task of squaring up a *three inch* long clubface to a target maybe 200 or more yards away is a difficult task. It is perhaps all right for most professionals although I have my doubts whether it is as accurate as my method. For a driver, for example, position the left foot so that an imaginary line from the ball which is approximately at right angles to the line through the ball to target, is passing just inside the left heel. Now place the right foot so that a line across both toes is directly on target. I do this by running my eyes along this line from right toe to left toe to target carefully but quickly, with my head turned (not tilted) to the left. You must, of course, use the club to gauge your distance from the ball. The last operation is to carefully place the clubhead

behind the ball so that the clubface (the bottom edge of the face) is at right angles to your toe line. I know from experience that this method lines up the body and clubface more accurately than any other. *Diagram 21b* shows a square clubface and the resulting pure backspin on the ball from a square impact with an on line swing. *Diagrams 21a and 21c* show closed and open clubfaces respectively, not at all desirable unless attempting purpose draw, hook, fade or slice.

I am not going to dwell on the open or closed stances, although I show them in *diagrams 20b and 20c*, except to say that they should only be used for producing special shots, and this book is dedicated to showing you how to produce the best shot of all – the straight one.

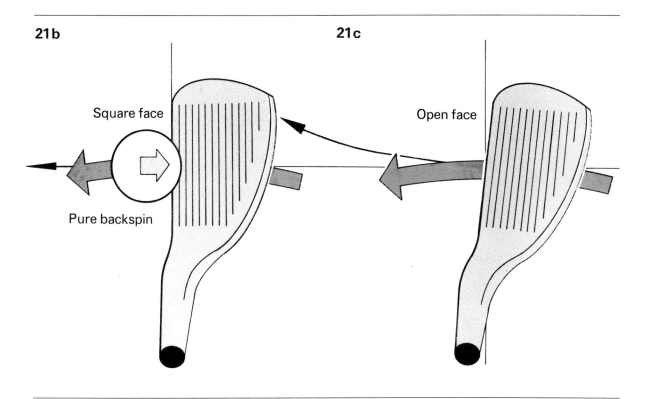

21b

Square face

Pure backspin

21c

Open face

Addressing the ball — the driver

Right shoulder
lower than left

right elbow tucked
back a little

Shaft and 'V' of left hand
point to left of chin

Bodyweight evenly
distributed on both
legs

Feet no further apart
than width of shoulders

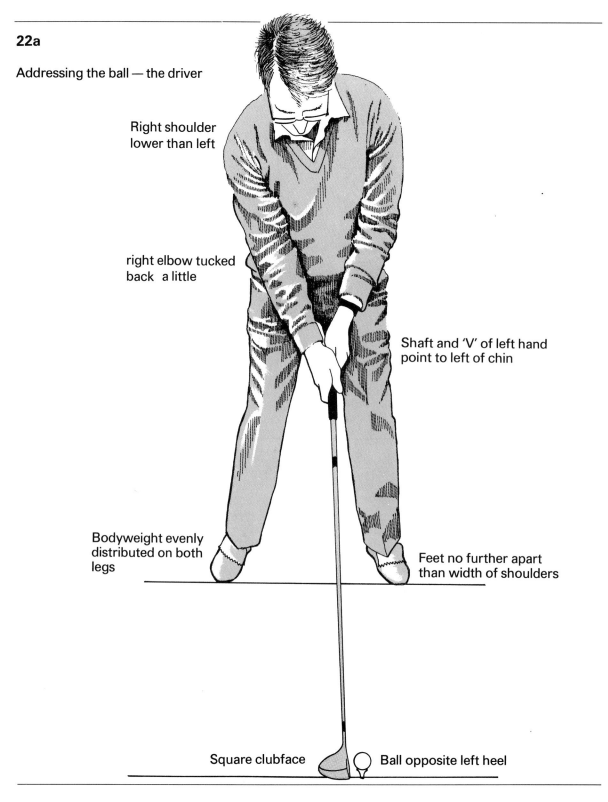

Square clubface   Ball opposite left heel

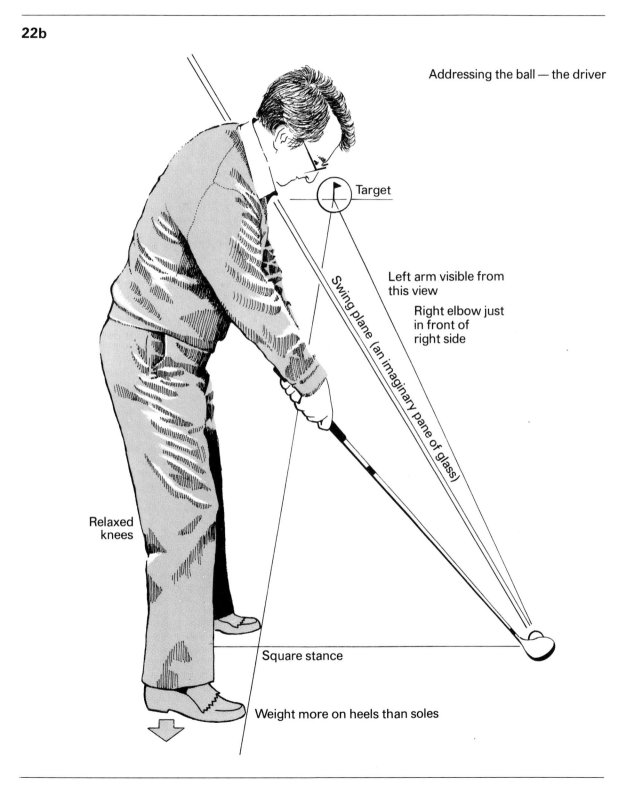

Addressing the ball — the driver

Target

Left arm visible from this view

Right elbow just in front of right side

Swing plane (an imaginary pane of glass)

Relaxed knees

Square stance

Weight more on heels than soles

Addressing the ball — short irons

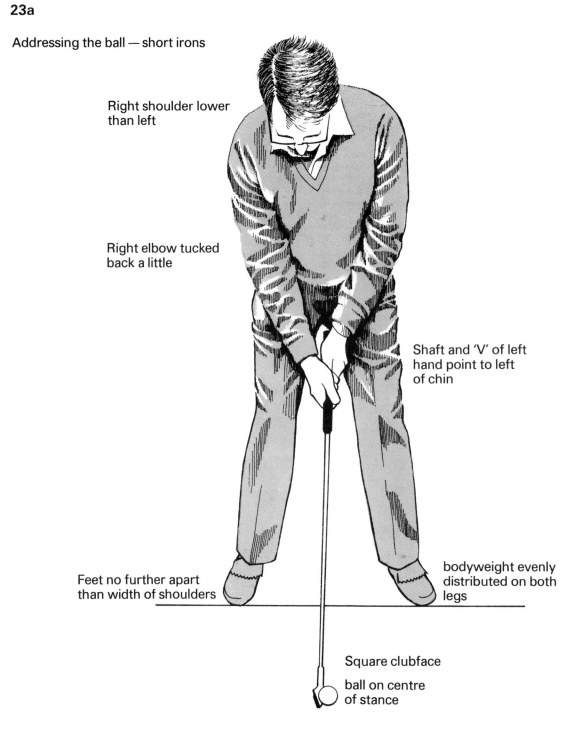

Right shoulder lower
than left

Right elbow tucked
back a little

Shaft and 'V' of left
hand point to left
of chin

Feet no further apart
than width of shoulders

bodyweight evenly
distributed on both
legs

Square clubface

ball on centre
of stance

To finalise this chapter study carefully the captioned *diagrams, 22 and 23* which show every aspect of the stance and address for the driver and for the short irons. Fairway woods and long irons are interpolated in between. I leave you with these illustrations as vivid pictures to bear in mind, but I must mention here that the swing plane was, to my knowledge, first put across by Ben Hogan in his book, "*The Modern Fundamentals of Golf*" as a large pane of glass, with a hole for the head, sitting on the shoulders and with the bottom edge sitting at the ball position and aimed at the target. We have Ben Hogan to thank for this "truth" which will last as long as the game does.

Some teachers like to get their pupils thinking of a railway line concept whereby the ball is on the outside line and the feet are on the inside line. Whilst I agree with this concept for the short shots from around the green because you are close enough to the target for the distance between "feet line" and ball to make a big difference, for shots further away it is quite sufficient and simpler to aim the line across the toes, the foot or feet line, directly at the target.

In more recent years a few well-known teachers have been advising an open stance for the standard shot, Lee Trevino for one, and Peter Alliss for another. Trevino, in fact, plays most of his shots with quite a strong open stance and uses a fade, a ball that curves to the right, but not strongly, for his standard shot. He can put purpose draw or even hook on a ball from this stance but he is not always successful. However, he does put quite a lot of stress on his back because from his very open stance he has to drop his right shoulder quite steeply under in relation to his "open" back in order to ensure that his swing is not strongly out-to-in in relation to the ball to target line. His swing is, however, strongly in-to-out in relation to his body. All this sounds complicated, but it does work for him. It is complicated and I do not recommend golfers to try

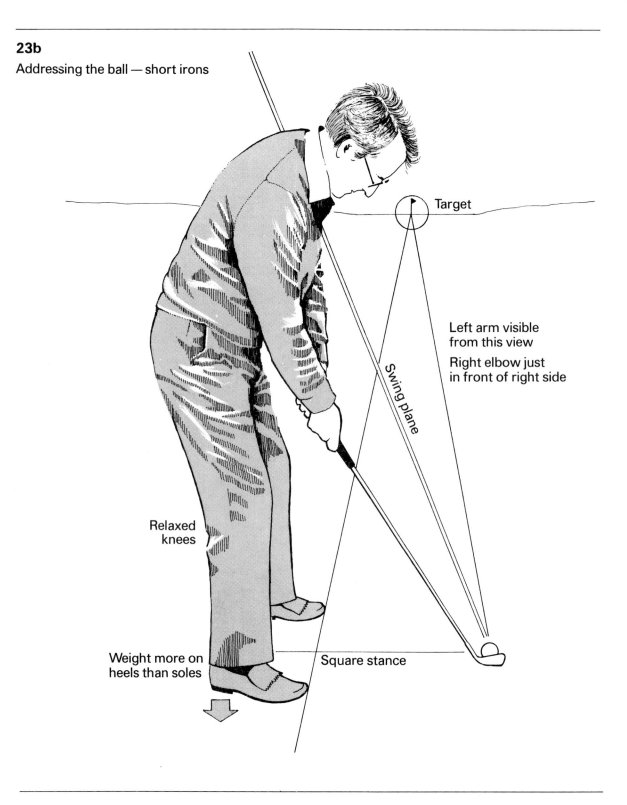

23b
Addressing the ball — short irons

Target

Left arm visible
from this view

Right elbow just
in front of right side

Swing plane

Relaxed
knees

Weight more on
heels than soles

Square stance

and follow it because in 99 out of 100 cases they will develop that awful complaint, the slice, and they will be causing it with out-to-in swings – very undesirable.

If you are a little on the plump side and a square stance creates difficulty in getting your hips through all you have to do is to adopt the square stance which I have described and then draw the left foot back an inch or two still keeping the shoulders and hips square *i.e.* aimed at the target.

To finalise I have one very important point to make, there is no excuse for a shot that is struck off line if it is due to poor lining up. I have occasionally seen top professionals hitting shots way off line after being careless and indifferent in taking their stance. My answer to that is use a more reliable method of lining up the body and clubface such as I describe, but do it carefully. *Study diagram 19 and fully understand that the two-flail system is contained within the clubhead "wheel", and must be first aimed at the target if it is to swing correctly on target.*

7: THE BACKSWING

The first stage of the backswing consists of taking the club back to approximately a horizontal position without any significant cocking or breaking of the wrists: the arms and club naturally in one piece. The triangle formed by the two arms and shoulders does not radically change its shape and the main reason for this is to get the axle and hub rotating as soon as possible in the slower part of the swing. Once these have been started off correctly, there is a good chance of continuing to the correct top position. You will discover that the left knee is extremely important in getting this axle pivot action moving nicely and that is why it is a key movement. Study the breakdown of the backswing in *diagram 24 and 25* very carefully and always remember that all parts of the swing must be put together in one smooth and rhythmical movement.

It is a good idea to practice the first stage on its own so that you stop at the end and check in a mirror that the back of the left hand and the clubface are facing forwards, also they should be just below the swing plane. The left arm should have hardly any separate movement of its own, only sufficient to enable the hands to move on the swing plane. Remember that the shoulders rotate on their own plane, which is flatter than the swing plane. The wrists should only break a little, but the axle has definitely rotated, initiated by the left knee. The left foot should stay firmly on the ground, the heel not rising until first stage is completed.

The whole objective of the backswing is to put the body and club into the best position at the top for a smooth, consistent downswing. The idea that some teachers have that the backswing is a wind-up action, which is released almost like a spring in the downswing, is misleading.

Let's be quite clear about it. The backswing is powered by the muscles of the legs and body, and the downswing is powered by similar muscles. These muscles must be given the correct messages both in the direction they must act and, even more important, how much and how little power they should exert at different moments of time.

The first rule, to be broken at your peril, is to perform the backswing at a leisurely pace. Only overdo this leisureliness in order to get to know the feel of wrongly using too much power. The downswing is the business part of the swing; keep your power for this section when playing and practising the correct swing.

A word of warning is necessary here on a common teaching fault. Do not take the clubface back square to the ball. Let it rotate so that at the end of the first stage it will have turned through a little less than 90°, a little less than a right angle. This is the correct clubface movement and does not lead to slicing as some teachers believe.

The backswing in its second stage is more simple than the first provided that the first stage has been reasonably, and correctly performed. The kinetic energy given to the clubhead during the first stage will help to keep it on its correct path, and the wrist cocking action of the left wrist, known by scientists as a radial deviation takes place partly under the influence of the force, provided the golfer does not interfere too much with the natural order of things. The wrists in *diagram 24 and 25* are shown cocking in this manner and the back of the left wrist stays slightly cupped, or flat with some golfers, all the way to the top. If you think of the knuckles of the left hand sliding under the pane of glass (the swing plane) you will be on the right track. Carrying out this action, even without a golf club, at the same time checking sideways on in a mirror is always good practice.

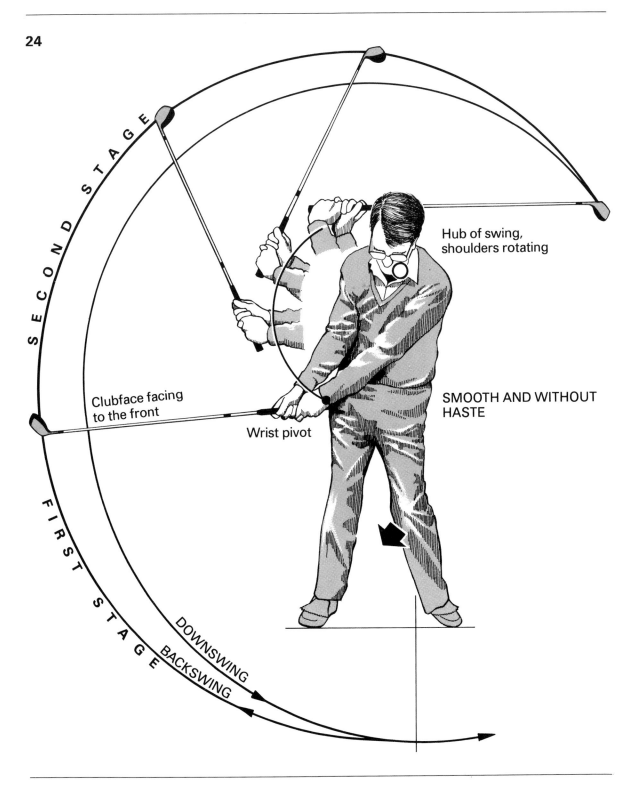

24

SECOND STAGE

FIRST STAGE

DOWNSWING

BACKSWING

Clubface facing
to the front

Wrist pivot

Hub of swing,
shoulders rotating

SMOOTH AND WITHOUT
HASTE

The left heel will rise off the ground, but should not rise too much, the hips will pivot till they are about 45° to the horizontal, and the shoulders will rotate until they have turned through approximately 90° when the back of the shoulders will be facing the target, as shown in *diagram 29* in the next chapter, the front view of the first stage of the downswing.

The stockily-built player may find it difficult to rotate the shoulders fully and this is not detrimental, provided he is not far from a full rotation. He will find also that his left heel will rise more than with a supple and slimmer golfer.

The clubshaft should reach, or nearly so, a horizontal position at the top of the swing, but if it is slightly short, or past the horizontal, it does not matter. However, if it is short it will point a little to the left of target and if it is past the horizontal it will point slightly right of target but this will only be so if you have cocked your wrists and rotated your shoulders correctly.

To get this backswing I want you to use a 12, 18 or 24-inch rule as an imaginary club to practise a slow-motion backswing, first and second stage. Check in the mirror using the flat of the ruler as the imaginary face of the clubhead. At the end of the first stage, when the ruler is horizontal, it's flat side should face forward together with the back of the left hand; it is then easy to move to the top and check the back of the left hand, the "clubface", and that the hands are immediately above the right shoulder, as shown in *diagram 25*.

25

Top of backswing

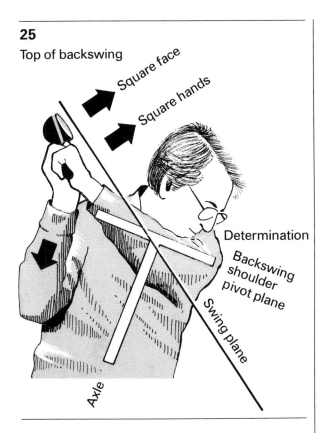

Square face

Square hands

Determination

Backswing shoulder pivot plane

Swing plane

Axle

AN EXTRAORDINARY MISCONCEPTION

Some teachers have got the idea that the clubface should stay square to its own line of flight just like a paddle in a paddle wheel. You can see how impossible this is by using *diagram 25* to put it into perspective. The hands would have to contort to an impossible degree to bring the clubface to this position, whereby the clubface would be pointing upwards along the swingplane. Try it! The true fact is that the clubface turns through 90°, or thereabouts, during the backswing, most of it taking place during the first stage. This leaves the clubface facing approximately square, at right angles to, the swing plane as shown in *diagram 25*. There are, as anyone would expect, variations especially among some of the more individualistic professionals but, without doubt, the best position for most golfers is when the clubface is square or perhaps a little open.

26a

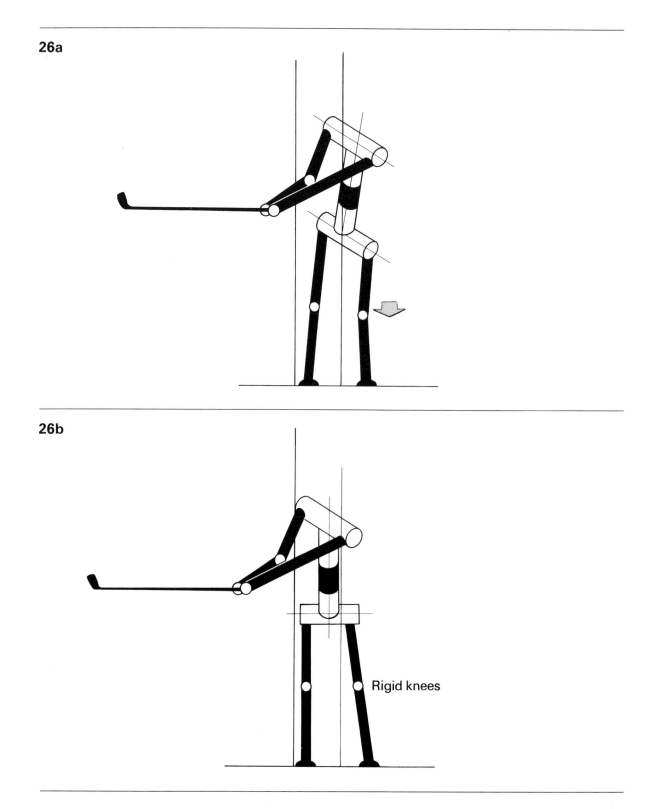

26b

Rigid knees

COMMON FAULTS

The three major errors committed by handicap golfers are (1) The left knee is bent directly forwards causing the right side to move away from the set-up position. (2) The left knee is kept too straight and immobile causing the trunk to sway to the right and further causing a lunging action of the shoulders during the downswing. (3) Too early and too much cocking of the wrists. Sketches of 1 and 2 in *diagrams 26a & b* should be sufficient to give you the picture. Fault number 3 is self-explanatory. You can if you like try them out. It does no harm to carry out a wrong movement because having felt it you know what you are up against and can more easily combat it.

SUMMARISING THE BACKSWING

1. Rotate the hub, elbows slightly relaxed, using key movement of left knee, and keeping the hub substantially in one position.
2. Arrive at the top in square or slightly open position on your own swing plane.
3. Do everything smoothly, rhythmically and leisurely, quietly if you prefer the word.
4. The wrists and hands should cock in a gradual swinging action. Your maxim should be SMOOTH and WITHOUT HASTE!

8: THE DOWNSWING

ONCE AGAIN, the most basic fact of all is that the golf swing is a rotational action and is a two-link flail system.

The first stage of the downswing has some similarities to the first stage of the backswing in so far as the shoulder joints are static. Therefore the rotation of the shoulders must be correctly planed or grooved in order to keep the hands and club below the swing plane. A common fault is to rotate your shoulders on the same plane as on the backswing as shown in *diagram 27a* immediately throwing the hands, followed by the clubhead, outside the swing plane. This is one of the main causes of the outside-to-in swing also shown in *diagram 27b*. Another major cause is an early uncocking of the wrists or throwing the clubhead from the top. I strongly advise you to test in slow motion the incorrect shoulder pivot so that you can see and feel what it is like to be wrong.

27a

Incorrect start to downswing.

The thicker line is the shoulder pivot plane for the backswing, which is at right angles to the spine.

When the initial shoulder rotation is on the same rotating plane as the backswing plane the hands will move outside the swing plane, this will cause the clubhead to also move out as it approaches impact. Crash! Crash! The damage is done and an out-to-in swing shown in diagram 27b is the result

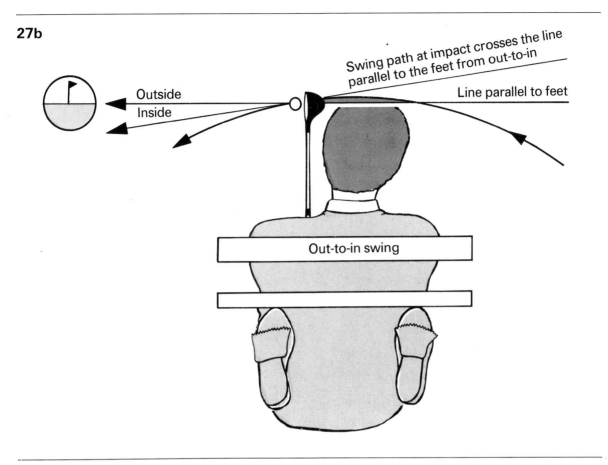

Swing path at impact crosses the line parallel to the feet from out-to-in

Line parallel to feet

Outside

Inside

Out-to-in swing

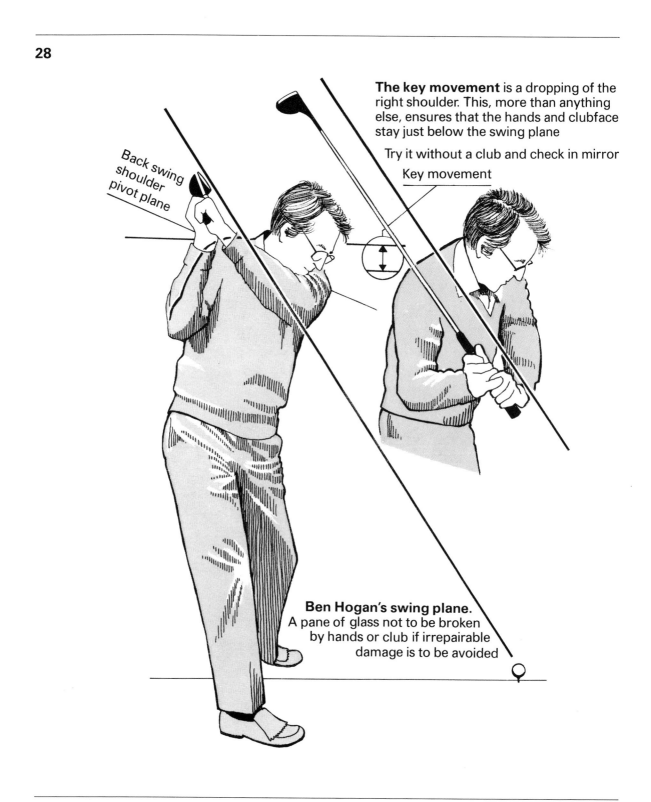

28

Back swing shoulder pivot plane

The key movement is a dropping of the right shoulder. This, more than anything else, ensures that the hands and clubface stay just below the swing plane

Try it without a club and check in mirror

Key movement

Ben Hogan's swing plane.
A pane of glass not to be broken
by hands or club if irreparable
damage is to be avoided

Now study the three drawings and notes, *diagrams 28, 29 and 30*, which strongly define the whole of the first stage in the downswing without too many words to cloud the picture.

Of course, this "stage one" of the downswing is fraught with danger. Guard against:
1. Rushing the start by allowing an almost overwhelming desire to get the clubhead down to the ball quickly to take charge.
   Cure: start gently.
2. Using the right hand too soon, known as throwing from the top.
   Cure: hold the right hand back or in other words, hold the wrist cock.
3. Pivoting the shoulders on the backswing shoulder pivot plane.
   Cure: drop that right shoulder just a fraction, and bring it under the chin in the second stage.

Practise the first stage in slow motion in front of a mirror front on and sideways on at any odd moment you have to spare. The integration of this with the rest of the swing as one smooth continuous swinging motion will come a little later when I describe the continuous swing exercise.

THE KEY MOVEMENT
This very important move shown in *diagram 28* should be practised in slow motion and at normal speed with a ruler and as a continuation of the backswing practise previously described. You will find that this move causes you to correctly slide your hips and then turn them. The sliding action of the hips will carry weight on to the left leg. It is far better, however, to think of shoulders rather than hips or legs. Dropping the right shoulder slightly will start them rotating on their correct plane, this is the KEY move.

Many professionals advocate, "Keep the right shoulder moving down and through, under the chin". Excellent, but you must not get the idea from this thought that golf is a right-sided or, for that matter, a left-sided game. It is, quite definitely, *not* either. It is a shoulder rotation game which during the downswing requires the muscles on the left side to stretch and the muscles on the right side to contract. You should now be well on the way to a complete picture of both the fact and the feel of the good swing.

It is most unfortunate, but nevertheless true, that the game has become overloaded and increasingly complicated by all kinds of teaching dogma. Yet the most simple and basic fact of all has been missed because scientific examination has only taken place in the last few years. And I say again that the results of these investigations have been largely ignored by teachers because they have already committed themselves to doctrines established by themselves, and it takes a rare kind of person who, not only admits he is wrong, but is also prepared to start all over again in his fundamental approach.

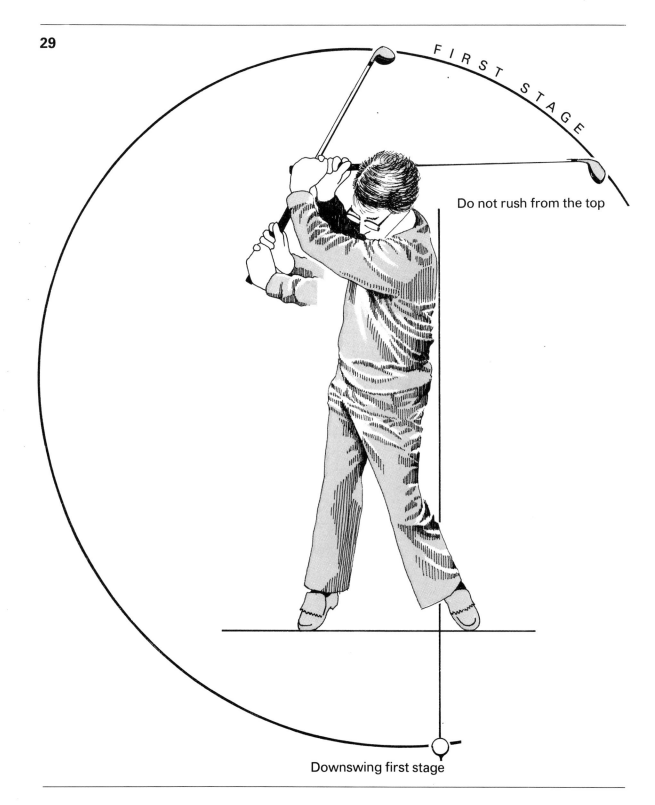

F I R S T S T A G E

Do not rush from the top

Downswing first stage

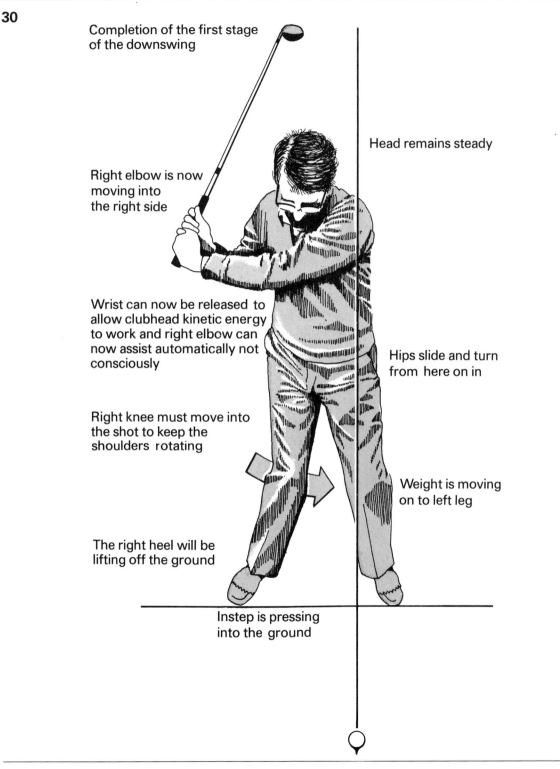

Completion of the first stage
of the downswing

Head remains steady

Right elbow is now
moving into
the right side

Wrist can now be released to
allow clubhead kinetic energy
to work and right elbow can
now assist automatically not
consciously

Hips slide and turn
from here on in

Right knee must move into
the shot to keep the
shoulders rotating

Weight is moving
on to left leg

The right heel will be
lifting off the ground

Instep is pressing
into the ground

The second stage of the downswing is much simpler to perform than the first provided that the first stage has been correct. The right leg should now be pushing quite powerfully, at the same time the wrist cock is released and the right hand begins to add its smaller power to the system by a pushing action from the right elbow. This right elbow power does not have to be put in consciously.

Control the hit impulse for a successful first stage performance and then in the second stage right elbow power will automatically release itself. The kinetic energy of the club-head is always there and if you don't interfere with it by a stiff wristed action, it will uncock the wrists for you. Your right hand must only assist, not overpower its action.

Yes, I know it is easier said than done, and that is why diligent and hard practise on the various exercises cannot be overdone. While all this is happening, the weight of the body will appear to be taken more and more on to the left leg with the hips sliding and rotating and the left side beginning to bow outwards.

As impact is approached, *diagrams 31 and 32*, the shoulders, the hub, must be kept rotating powerfully with the right shoulder moving under the chin as shown in *diagram 33*. By the way, one of the secrets of long hitting is this ability to keep the hub rotating powerfully through the impact position. A fault into which some golfers, particularly in the higher handicap range, sometimes fall is what is known by teachers as quitting on the shot. This is simply a slowing-up, indeed almost stopping of the shoulder rotation, as though the golfer is obsessed with hitting the ball with his hands and arms alone. This is a sure way of decelerating the clubhead at impact and therefore losing power and distance.

Always remember that it is the legs and body muscles which supply most of the power in rotating the shoulders so keep them moving through impact, smoothly and with authority

and confidence. It is very important to do this and FORGET any thought of whipping the hands through impact.

In fact, most of the golfers who think or believe that the hands are a large source of power in the so-called hitting area, never experience the wonderful feeling of "tapping" a ball on the sweet-spot a surprisingly long way up the middle, with a smooth, easy body movement and amazingly little hand power. I call this the "Theo Tap" because it literally amounts to tapping the ball away with such apparently little power the golfer gives himself quite a shock. Many of my pupils will bear witness to this touch of magic.

The main point is this. The older person, by this I mean people past the age of 25 or perhaps 30, if he is told to hit hard from the beginning will automatically destroy the efficiency of the two lever flail by throwing the clubhead too soon. In other words, he will use his hands too much and too soon and the clubhead will not speed up as it should do. He will also tend to pivot his shoulders incorrectly, probably resulting in the right shoulder coming out and round, instead of down and under, producing an out-to-in swing.

It is unfortunately this overwhelming desire to get the clubhead to the ball which is set alight by being told to hit hard from the very start of instruction. I am quite convinced in my own mind that this "hit hard" theory has destroyed the potential ability of many a bright pupil. What is needed is something to restrain the desire to hit and not to explode it.

Approaching impact front view

Keep the shoulders
rotating don't
'quit on the shot'

Left side is
bowing
outwards,
hips are
turning
as well as
sliding.

The clubhead is now under strong influence
of centrifugal force with right elbow assisting,
but not overpowering it

Clubhead really
accelerates

Right knee is pushing
and right heel rising
well off the ground
in order to keep
shoulders rotating
smoothly

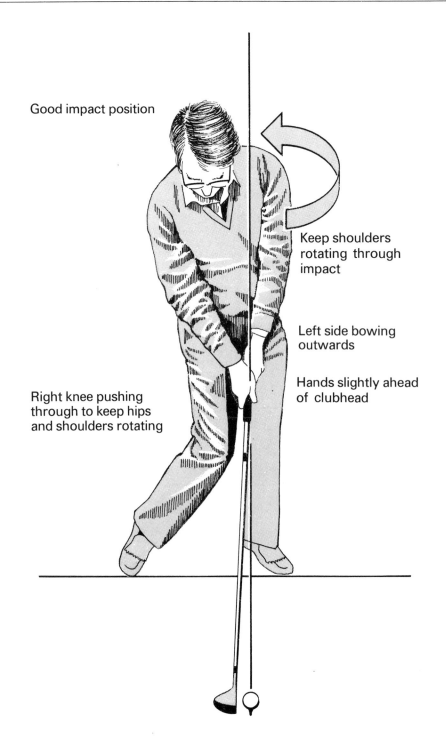

Good impact position

Keep shoulders
rotating through
impact

Left side bowing
outwards

Hands slightly ahead
of clubhead

Right knee pushing
through to keep hips
and shoulders rotating

Good impact position

Right shoulder moving
under chin

Left arm visible
from this view

Shoulder pivot plane
through impact should
be kept within this range

THE COMPLETE DOWNSWING AND THE "THEO TAP"

The complete downswing, as performed by a stick man, is shown in *diagram 34*. This diagram is worth a great deal of study, always bearing in mind that the hands and clubhead are moving on their own tilted circles on the swing plane.

The "Theo Tap" is a practise which is design-

34

The downswing of the stickman

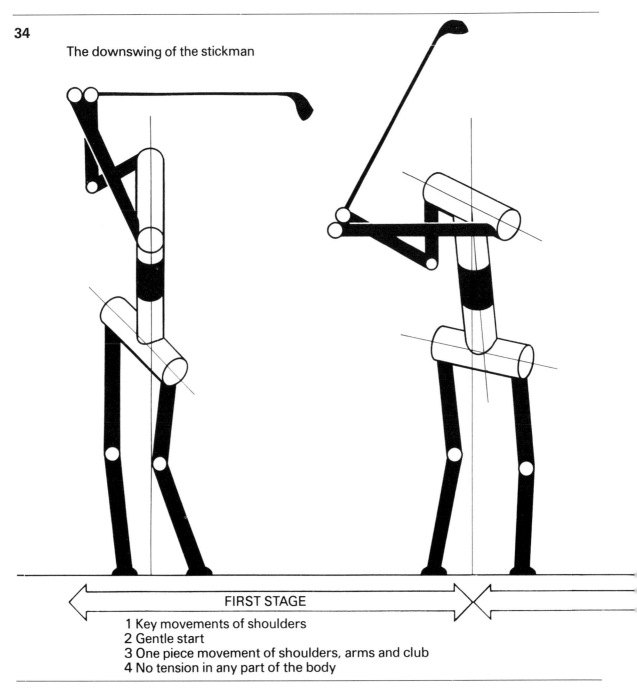

FIRST STAGE

1 Key movements of shoulders
2 Gentle start
3 One piece movement of shoulders, arms and club
4 No tension in any part of the body

ed to show you a really efficient two-flail swing with an absolute minimum of input power. It is diametrically opposed to the hit-it-hard brigade. On the practice ground pick a target about 150 yards away and with a three wood or three IRON try very hard to literally "tap" a teed-up ball on to the spot. It is essential to start the downswing gently and to not cast or throw from the top. Let the clubhead drag behind at the start of the

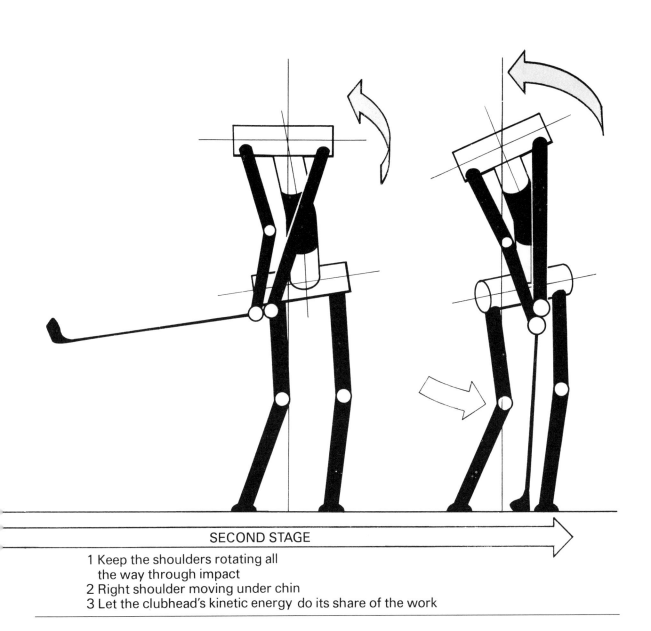

SECOND STAGE

1 Keep the shoulders rotating all
   the way through impact
2 Right shoulder moving under chin
3 Let the clubhead's kinetic energy do its share of the work

downswing. The clubhead through impact must be moving towards the target. If you previously had a strong out-to-in swing you will feel for some time that your swing is on an in-to-out line.

Above all, feel that you are using no more than 70% of full power and you and I will really be getting somewhere when you can write to me saying you are amazed how far the ball flies with so little power. Another vital sensation is of freewheeling through impact, a wonderful feeling to achieve consistently. That is what this two-flail system is all about.

The "Theo Tap" exercise is confined to the practice ground because it requires real golf balls. The following routines can all be done in your garden, on any space which will take a full swing, and are designed to enhance your timing, rhythm and general feel of the swing. They will also iron out a particular fault. Perform them for a few minutes every day and as a preliminary to the "Theo Tap" drill.

The first exercise is the full continuous swing and consists of two-handed full swings, linked continuously together, back and forward, back and forward, with an easy grace. Starting at the address position, you take a normal backswing, downswing and follow through. Then, without stopping at the end of the follow through, you return to the top of the backswing via the address position in one slow, smooth action. Go into the downswing and so on for several swings. Not many seconds will elapse before you begin to feel tired, so a few minutes of this practise every day or so will be quite sufficient. There are several purposes for which this exercise is designed and I list them in order of importance:
1. For an easy smooth rhythm.
2. For a gentle start to the downswing.
3. For keeping the clubhead moving towards the target through impact area.
4. For keeping the shoulders rotating through impact and so that the right shoulder moves under the chin and not "out and around".
5. For getting to a "square" position at the top of the backswing.
6. For getting to a good follow through completion position (the follow through is dealt with in detail in the next chapter).

Point 5 can be checked by occasionally looking at your reflection in a window as you complete your backswing and checking that the hands are vertically above the right shoulder, the back of the left hand is on the swing plane and reasonably flat or slightly cupped. The shaft should be pointing at the target and the clubface is roughly parallel to or lying on the swing plane at approx. 60°, or a little less, to the horizontal. This angle applies to woods, see *diagram 25*, which also shows the kind of picture you should see reflected in the window sideways on.

The above swing routine performs another important role. It keeps the muscles in trim and good swing working order during the week in readiness for the weekend game. Believe me, you will be able to swing a club more easily when you arrive on the first tee on Saturday morning. It must be remembered that top-line professionals take great care not to ruin their performances by heavy gardening work and other back-wrecking jobs. The average club golfer, however, cannot ignore these tasks; they must be done. So it is well worthwhile spending time on continuous swinging, particularly as it only takes a few minutes.

I have been asked, "Why make these exercises continuous?". There are several reasons, but the most important one is that you can feel the swing being grooved, because of the very nature of continuously swinging. Secondly, the single swing extends in time for no more than one and a half seconds which makes it difficult for the brain to pick up and store vital knowledge of timing and rhythm in such a short space of time. Thirdly, several swings, all closely following one another without a break, are much more easily monitored and compared with each other.

Other continuous swing practises can supplement this line of thought. If you find whilst carrying out the drill that the head moves about which means you are swaying, try continuous swinging with the feet about six inches apart. This narrow base will stop you hitting too hard from the top, and will help to prevent you from swaying about. If you do, you'll fall flat on your face. It also helps to develop good knee movement where the two knees alternatively cock forwards and inwards, first the left on the backswing and then the right on the downswing.

Other good homework exercises are swinging one-handed, first with the left and then with the right. Make sure, however, that both hands move so that the clubface opens through approximately 90° in the backswing, returns to square at impact, and closes approximately 90° during the following through, a total movement (rotation) of 180°. Some of you may feel that your hands are slightly rolling or turning to bring the clubface to its correct positions. Your maxim for the downswing should be *"Don't rush from the top, let the clubhead work."*

At this point it will pay you to study the major factors that emerged from the true dynamics of the downswing which we looked at earlier.

1. A gentle start is essential, firstly to help you not to cast or hit from the top and, secondly, it helps to ensure better timing by delaying the wrist release position.
2. It is important not to hold the club in a vice-like grip. If you grip the club too hard you inhibit the action of centrifugal force, the action which naturally uncocks the wrists.
3. Rotating the shoulders, the hub of the swing, smoothly and gracefully about the top of a stationary spine during the downswing is the first essential in feeding power into the clubhead. The muscles in the legs and back which set the shoulder rotation in motion are the most powerful in the body and do not need to work at full blast on top speed to be at their most efficient output.
4. To take an almighty wallop at the ball is an almost uncontrollable natural instinct. It is, without doubt, the most difficult psychological factor to overcome. Control yourself and your timing problems will disappear. You will be much better off if you not only start gently in the downswing but if you also allow the wrists to cock more fully after the shoulders and arms move into the downswing. In fact, the best swingers of a golf club allow the drag inertia of the clubhead to do this for them.
5. Never forget that hand leverage plays a minor part in the power train for obtaining all-important clubhead speed, and, above all, the hands must assist centrifugal force, not take over its work. Hand leverage, which is mainly right elbow power, need only be applied during the middle third of the downswing but most golfers do not need to apply it consciously. It is usually automatic. Try to achieve the feeling that Faldo seems to have when hitting his best shots. He freewheels through impact.
6. Never lose touch with the overall sense of rhythm and smoothness necessary to transmit the power of the muscles into clubhead speed. Even a train of gear wheels needs oiling to keep them running smoothly. So relax a little.

9: THE FOLLOW THROUGH

35

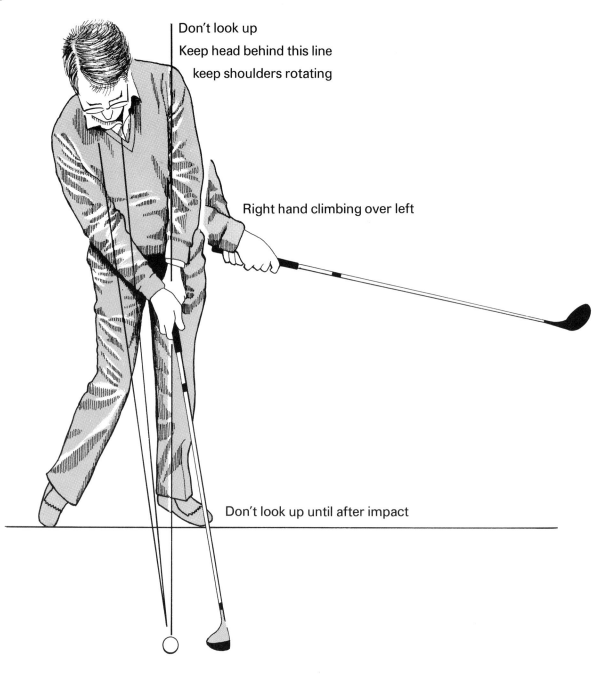

Don't look up

Keep head behind this line

keep shoulders rotating

Right hand climbing over left

Don't look up until after impact

Whilst it is possible to hit good shots with a bad follow through, it is true to say that a bad follow through makes it difficult to be a consistently good striker of the ball. It is surprising how few people realise that the follow through is very similar to the downswing when it comes to the position of the clubface and the hands in relation to the swing plane. In some respects, the follow through is a mirror image of the downswing as the sketches show and its main purpose is to extract all the energy of the swing after impact with the ball.

In reality the follow through is a natural extension of the downswing with the legs, shoulders and arms moving smoothly into a perfect patter of completion. My full continuous routine demonstrates that the swing can be concluded naturally. And now study *diagram 35* and the notes which go with it.

As you go into the ball and make contact keep looking at the spot on the ground where it was even though you are already well into the follow through. Another important factor is that by keeping the shoulders rotating the golfer will hold the clubface reasonably square for a few inches after impact. It is then that the clubface will begin to turn over and close as the left elbow bends.

A good completion to the follow through is shown in *diagram 36*. Where at the end of the follow through the clubface lies on the swing plane but facing backwards. There is a strong sense of mirror image about the hands and the clubface. There is also a certain logic behind it, particularly when looking at the swing from a mechanical point of view.

Remember that the clubface during the down-swing has turned through 90° as previously described. After impact the clubface turns a further 90°, most of which takes place in the first half of the follow through. It is a great help to know exactly how the follow through should finish and often it ensures a good downswing by getting to a correct finish, particularly a high hands, square clubface finish.

I sometimes put pupils into the classic high hands completion position and then ask them to attempt to arrive at this position by free-wheeling through impact. The results are often quite fantastic with shots zooming away.

I cannot count the number of times I have heard someone say after a bad shot, "You looked up". It is all too easy to blame a bad shot on a simple statement like this, and leave it there as if it solves everything. It is, in fact, a catch phrase which relieves the adviser of all further responsbility, which requires no further analysis, or so the pundits think. Indeed, "looking-up" (usually an attempt to see the ball in flight too soon) can cause a number of indifferent shots. It takes a real expert to analyse these properly, but then only with slow motion playback on video tape or film. Without doubt the most common result from looking-up is a topped shot or in the extreme case an air shot, the complete miss. However, the expert golfer can easily look up and hit perfect shots by keeping the primary pivot at the neck, the shoulder pivot, in a fixed position.

I say again the full continuous swing routine will groove the perfect follow through. You must work hard at this. It's most crucial to the new game you are building.

High hands finish

Swing plane

A common fault among beginners is to spin the right foot 'out and around' causing an 'out to in' swing.

Right foot up on toe Never pass the vertical

At this point I want you to look at the angles of attack at which a clubface meets the ball. *Diagram 37* shows the angle most desirable for the driver striking a ball off a tee peg, fairways woods striking a ball off the ground, and for irons. The main difference between woods and irons is that sweeping the ball away is the best thought to have for the woods whereas it is much better to take a slight divot after the ball with all iron shots from grass, ball first, turf next so to speak. Nevertheless, it is still satisfactory to sweep the irons away, although the ball/turf concept of hitting the ball on the downswing, does create more backspin.

It is worth recording for you that all shots have backspin ranging from the driver at something like 60 revolutions per second to the pitching wedge (No.10 iron) at about 180 (11000 rpm). There is no such thing as topspin or overspin on a golf ball struck by the clubhead. Some pundits say that drawn and hooked shots have topspin because the clubface moves over the ball on an in-to-out flight path. This belief is totally untrue. Every shot has tremendous backspin and is kept in the air by this spin which creates more pressure on the underside and less pressure on the top side of the ball. This is well known in the studies of golf ball aerodynamics.

The effects of spin on ball flight are very similar to those in the table tennis world. For instance, the topspin shot quickly dips downwards on to the table whereas backspin lifts the ball away from the surface. If it were possible to hit a golf ball into the air with topspin (which it isn't) it would not travel more than a few yards. And that's the truth which destroys another myth of this game.

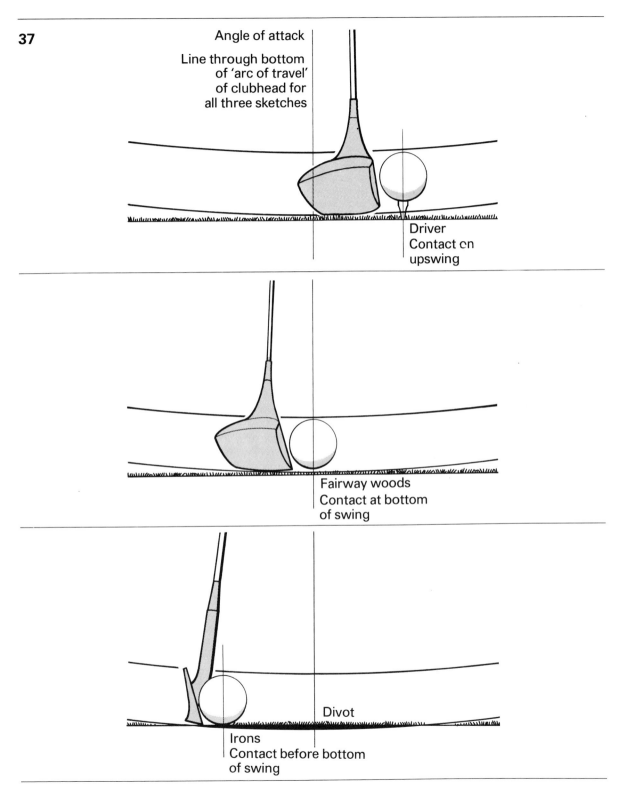

37

Angle of attack

Line through bottom
of 'arc of travel'
of clubhead for
all three sketches

Driver
Contact on
upswing

Fairway woods
Contact at bottom
of swing

Divot

Irons
Contact before bottom
of swing

10: PSYCHOLOGY OF THE SWING

The statement that "golf is all in the mind" has been repeated billions of times yet rarely has anyone understood the proper significance of this well-worn catch phrase within the context of the true dynamics of the swing. We must face the facts. For the majority of players the golf swing is a continuing mystery. Indeed, the conception and design of the club is not in line with the truth. Here in the 1980s, the age of the microchip, some golf club manufacturers are still designing clubs in the belief that the shaft whips into the ball at impact and therefore its own flex and torque adds substantially to the ball's initial speed. So they attempt to make clubs with a shaft flexing characteristic tuned to the swing. It is time for all manufacturers to apply the correct science and discover that the shaft bends forwards to its maximum degree just *before* impact and therefore does *not* add anything to the transfer of energy at impact.

This and many other scientific facts are available to the golf trade, and should be incorporated in the design of equipment to help everyone play a better game. For instance, the psychology of the game should be drawn from this new knowledge so everything really does make sense, and is in line with the true dynamics of the swing. The golfer is bound to benefit tremendously, and consequently the game's standard will improve.

At the moment, I feel that I am a lone voice. I want people to know the truth. I want people to play golf as an *applied* science and not as a hit and miss exercise.

HOW TO THINK OF RETAINING THE WRIST COCK ANGLE

"Pull down with your left hand as though you are pulling a bell rope" is perhaps one of the most common ideas. I prefer to go further. It is, in my opinion, very important to feel the clubhead lagging behind, and in turn feel the back of the right hand trying to touch the right forearm. For you these are perhaps new sensations but they cannot happen unless your grip is light and the downswing is started gently. The time to search for this awareness is when you are working on the continuous swing exercises out on the practice ground or at home using those plastic balls which are full of holes.

The gentle start to the downswing is a must. I have known single figure players who, when attempting to reduce power in order to increase the efficiency of my two-flail system, have still "thrown from the top". This, of course, means that their timing was way out and it was impossible for them to get any reasonable clubhead speed until they learned to *leave the clubhead behind* so that it builds up its own energy and accelerates fast into impact. Think again about the ruler test and its important teachings.

THOUGHTS FOR KEEPING THE CLUBHEAD ON LINE AT IMPACT

Swinging the clubhead on line to target is obviously one essential for a straight shot. The reminder of just how things should be done can be found in *diagram 38*. My studies reveal that a high percentage of handicap golfers swing across the line from out-to-in, and a high percentage of professionals swing in-to-out.

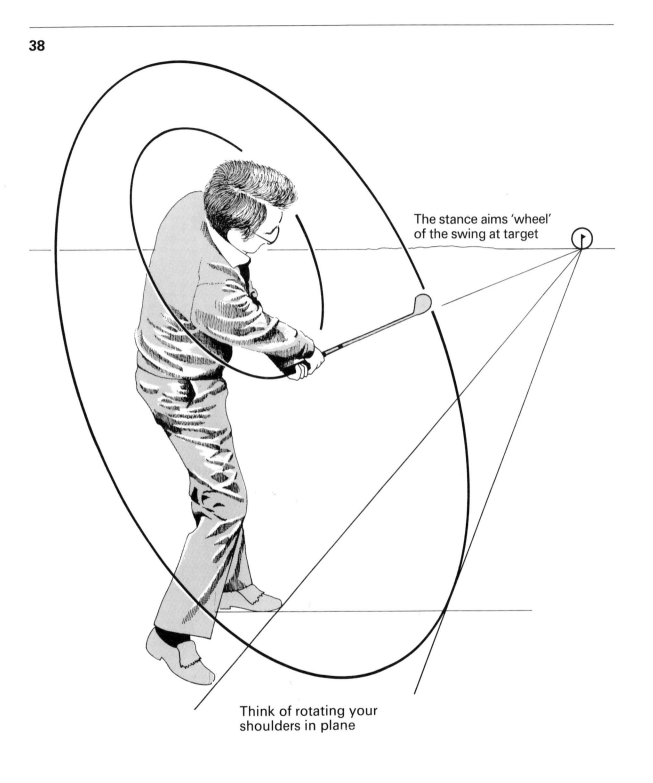

38

The stance aims 'wheel' of the swing at target

Think of rotating your shoulders in plane

Therefore, the statement, "few people hit straight shots" is true. The handicapper has no reason to swing out-to-in, and, indeed, usually wishes he could swing straight. The professional's in-to-outer produces a controlled draw for most of the time, but it is when this draw becomes an uncontrolled hook that he wishes he could swing consistently straight.

My view is that everyone right from the start should learn to swing on line and at the same time know what it feels like to go in-to-out and out-to-in with the certain knowledge that they are doing so. I am aware that many golfers believe that the slight draw gives them maximum distance, but in practice it does not work this way. Hogan, Trevino, Nicklaus, and others with the master's touch developed a fade for greater accuracy and control. I fail to understand why some of them seem to think that the straight shot is the most difficult in the book. I have proved it beyond doubt that the straight ball is not difficult to produce and in the long run is the most satisfying and productive. It is the consistent base from which to develop the purpose fade and draw.

Swinging the clubhead on line with a correctly aimed body alignment is the first and most obvious result of a correctly performed downswing. The following trigger thoughts are ways of achieving this. Only one thought at any time is necessary but try them all separately to find which is best for you. Then it may be necessary when things go wrong to change from time to time to get a new thought working for you.
1. Gentle start to downswing.
2. Right shoulder down, under, and through.
3. Leave clubhead behind at start of downswing.
4. Forget everything else and think only of leaving a slight mark on the grass which either points at target or *slightly* to the right of it.

THOUGHTS FOR GETTING THE CLUBFACE SQUARE

A mistake made by many beginners, and sometimes more experienced players, is that they try to swing in a direction opposed to where a curving flight finishes. Let me explain. Take the example of the player with a bad slice. He will often try to swing the club more and more to the left of target in the mistaken belief that this will automatically steer the ball away from trouble. In this case the swing becomes more and more out-to-in and the clubface is more and more open. The slice becomes more aggravated and the results more and more depressing.

There are two basic faults which must be cured. Firstly, the swing, and secondly, the open clubface at impact. The major reason for this last fault, and this has not been fully understood by teachers, is gripping too hard, as I have previously explained and as the ruler test clearly shows. The following is a list (in order of importance) of thoughts for curing the open clubface fault.
1. Grip lightly, even loosely.
2. Feel as though you are slapping the ball with the back of the left hand or if you prefer the palm of the right.
3. If everything else fails, rotate the hands anticlockwise through impact. In other words, climb the right hand over the left so that the clubface is well closed soon after impact.

If the cures have worked properly you should finish up feeling that you are swinging towards the trouble side of the fairway and freewheeling through the ball.

Most professionals and a fair number of low handicap players and a few high handicappers, have been troubled at some time with an uncontrollable hook. In some cases, the hook is pulled to the left by the right shoulder coming out and around – this is a "pulled hook". A shut or closed clubface to its own line of travel gives the ball hook spin, and even a swing that is on line to target will result in the ball starting off to the left and then curving further into trouble.

How then do you stop the clubface coming into the ball closed or shut? Many professionals try what they call blocking the left side, a somewhat complicated procedure which later on can easily give rise to other problems.

The easiest and most sensible method is to stop hitting so hard with the hands, particularly the right one. Once gain try to develop a strong feeling of freewheeling through impact. The cure is as simple as that.

THE MOST VALUABLE THOUGHT OF ALL
The scientists in their book, *The Search for the Perfect Swing*, said, ''The hub in the mind, a vivid image of the hub of the swing lined up to turn in a plane through the target is a great help to swinging in-plane''. This thought is an ideal foundation stone for the whole pattern of the structure of thought processes. It is a base from which to build up an excellent psychological approach to the game for the reason that golfers are two-flail systems and the primary action of such a system is the rotation of the hub (the shoulders).

Thinking of rotating your shoulders ''in plane to target'' is the most basic thought because of its association with the mechanical fact that in the two flail system the first pivot point is from where most of the power comes. An extension of this thought is to think of the hands as being the rim of a wheel which is turning in plane to target. *Diagram 38* illustrates this thought process in pictorial form and note that the left arm forms a spoke of the wheel, which is rotating in plane, or in line if you prefer, with the target.

A THOUGHT FOR GIVING YOU A GOOD FOLLOW THROUGH
Many older players complain that they have a follow through which feels choked or incomplete and are aware of the fact that it is affecting their striking of the ball. How many times have you read or heard the statement that it does not matter what you do with the follow through once you have hit the ball?

Forget it. It is so misleading, particularly to the novice. It is, in fact, quite difficult to hit good shots with a bad follow through. Take for example the player whose follow through is very short. His hands, we will assume, only reach hip height. The chances are that his clubhead has already begun to slow down before impact in order for the hands to come to a stop so soon after hitting the ball. This means he is losing distance because clubhead speed at impact is too low. Try this thought: Keep the shoulders rotating through impact. This will not only help to keep the clubhead speed high, it will also help to keep it on line. A warning, however, to the older player. Care should be taken not to damage muscles by making them do something to which they are not fully accustomed. Bring them into action carefully.

THE FINAL FORMULA
The way to success is to have a picture of a smooth controlled, yet powerful two-flail action. And this is the formula:
1. From a square stance the whole movement, backswing, downswing and follow through must be smooth, rhythmical, and full.
2. The shoulders must pivot around a spine that does not sway like a tree in the wind.
3. The backswing should be a leisurely thing right into the first few inches of the downswing, and if relaxing the grip a little helps you to keep the wrists cocked for the first part of the downswing, then RELAX them.
4. Pivot your shoulders during the downswing on a plane that points at the target (see *diagram 38*), and keep the

hands and clubhead slightly below the swing plane, during the first part of the downswing.

5. Be relaxed all through the swing, yet still feel in control. Tension destroys smoothness.
6. The golf swing is a progression of muscle power and so are the movements that derive from it.

The power of the body must be applied in close progression, beginning with the legs, followed by the hips, shoulders, arms and hands. Never forget that the last link of power, the hands as a unit, is needed only to *assist* centrifugal force and should not be used to overcome this vital and natural force. Indeed, those players who do overcome this force use their hands too much and cannot be described as true swingers. Generally speaking, these hitters are the people who find golf more difficult as they get older and the years take their toll of physical co-ordination. Whatever the individual situation, the finest method of practising is the continuous swing exercise, bringing into action the above formula stage by stage.

There is, and always will be, only one real secret to better golf and I discovered it more than 15 years ago. Now I have given it to you. I ask you to learn about the true dynamics of the swing by reading this book several times if necessary, while, at the same time, diligently carry out the various tests and exercises I have given so that you can feel the truth in your mind and body.

11: THE LAST SHOT

39

The final objective

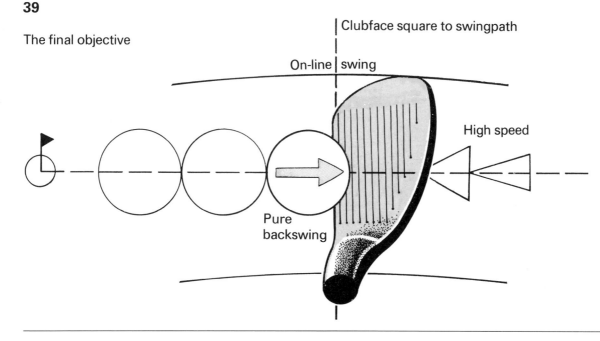

Clubface square to swingpath

On-line swing

High speed

Pure backswing

Maybe I lost a few friends when I declared that Sevvy Ballesteros did not understand or fully appreciate the reasons and mechanics of why he is able to make so many fine shots that make him such a fine striker of the ball. Now I end with a criticism of Jack Grout, friend and mentor of Jack Nicklaus and noted one of the best teachers in the world.

But first let me say that I began this book by discussing and dismissing a number of important misconceptions all of which are associated with the actual swing and I did so deliberately to clear the way so to speak before presenting the truth. I guided you firstly through the dynamics of the swing, and then through the various components of the swing building them around the two-flail system. My objective has been to provide you with an ON LINE TO TARGET swing which delivers the clubface to the ball square and with a sensible angle of attack, see *diagram 39*. The result is a straight shot with pure backspin.

It is not difficult, of course, to nominate the type of swing which produces this shot by using the way the ball flies as the main guide. It is much more difficult for the average golfer to analyse what kind of swing produces a draw, a hook, a fade or a slice unless he knows exactly what happens at impact. It is in this technical area of teaching that there is so much confusion and bewilderment. Let me explain. A number of well-known instructors have got some strange and incorrect ideas of impact and ball flight.

And, here I return to Jack Grout, author of "Let me teach you golf as I taught Jack Nicklaus". He states: "For as long as you play golf remember this: your shot will always start out in the direction your clubhead was moving during impact. If your clubhead was cutting from inside to outside the line the ball must at least start out to the right of target". A little later he says: "The initial direction in which a golf shot takes off is determined primarily by

40

Another misconception

The ball directions shown are incorrect

Clubface open to swingpath
(points to the right of the swingpath)

Clubface closed to swingpath
(points to the left of the swingpath)

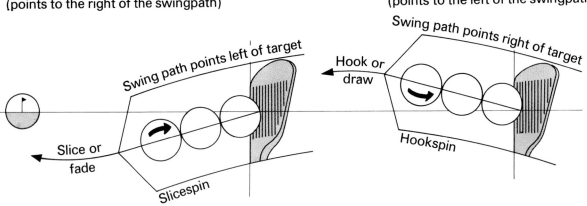

41a

What really happens when the clubface
is not square to the swingpath at impact

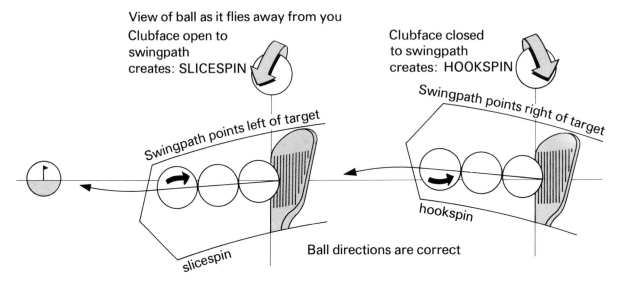

the path on which the clubhead is moving when it releases the ball".

I am sorry that I have to contradict such an eminent teacher but I do so in the interest of truth. But, firstly, let me show Jack Grout's theory in sketch form to clearly show what he means. See *diagram 40* – the two drawings show the ball starting out in the direction of the swingpath.

Let me correct this misconception. Look at *diagrams 41a & b* which show four different impact situations and illustrates the real truth. It shows that the ball begins its flight much nearer to where the clubface is pointing than where the swingpath swings. It also explains the way the ball spins e.g. hookspin and slicespin.

Now back to the final objective, *diagram 39*. In the classic swing of a top class professional, such as Nick Faldo, the clubhead approaches the ball at about 120 mph. On impact with the ball the clubhead is slowed down to something like 98 mph. At this stage the ball and clubhead are travelling together at this speed for about three quarters of an inch. Then the ball which has now been somewhat flattened on one side begins to push itself away from the clubface. This action from the ball, which can be called bounce, slows down the clubhead still further to perhaps 86 mph. At the same time the ball accelerates to about 155 mph. These figures are approximate, vary from golfer to golfer, but they give you a general picture of the interface between clubhead and ball. And, just for good measure, I would like you to appreciate from these figures that the ball almost doubles its speed at impact due to its own coefficient of restitution, bounce in simple language.

All this maybe scientific jargon to some of you but there is no denying it is all part of the magic of golf and the TRUTH.

41b

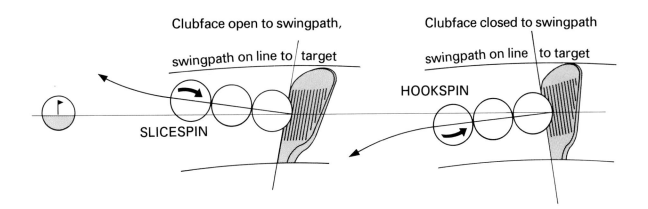

Clubface open to swingpath,

swingpath on line to target

SLICESPIN

Clubface closed to swingpath

swingpath on line to target

HOOKSPIN

12: PUTTING THE BALL DOWN

The last shot in this game of ours is the putt, be it 20 feet, two feet or two inches and until the ball drops into the hole we cannot exclaim, "It's your honour" or "That's all square" or "That putt puts me one under my handicap for the round". Some people describe putting as the most controversial part of golf and they could be right. Putting styles vary from individual to individual much more than in tee and fairway shots. Most golfers use a grip which is very similar to the one they use for other shots. They may have small differences, for example the first finger of the right hand (right-handed players) is sometimes placed so that it reaches down the handle instead of wrapping around it. Other players have found that reversing the hand position, placing the left hand below the right, gives them better results. There are so many variations in grip, stance and method of applying the putter to the ball that it would be unwise to attempt to describe them all.

Many young golfers use a wristy action, but some find, if they get into top class professional play, that the wristy action is too susceptible to the "yips" when the pressure is on. The yips is a slang term for a nervous reaction which twitches the hands and ruins the putt. Golfers who have never suffered from this complaint are sometimes cynical or disdainful about it, but then they can afford to be. They should consider themselves lucky and appreciate the fact that mental pressures can be quite tremendous when faced with the task of "sinking this one for the Open championship". Notice the fact that people who have become agitated often have trembling hands, which they find difficult to control.

My advice, therefore, as regards hand action in putting is to develop a style which eliminates conscious wrist action whereby the muscles of the forearms are not asked to control the movement of the club. You are more liable to become a consistently good putter if you lock your wrists and use your arms, shoulders and hands in one piece (no relative movement between them). At the same time, make quite sure that the legs and hips do not move, so that the only pivot in the system is at the top of the spine, the shoulder pivot in other words.

A few of you may have already decided that a wristy action is a must for you despite everything I have said. For you I strongly recommend that an extremely light grip should be used for the shorter putts of say nine feet or less, combined with a pendulum action using the left wrist as a hinge. The feeling for this kind of action is to let the club dangle with as light as possible gripping pressure from the hands. Then to swing the club with the hands only, rather like a pendulum with the top of the pendulum, the pivot that is, being the hands and wrists.

There is no doubt, of course, that much of the success of good putting derives from the correct mental approach and such things as determination, concentration and the will to get the ball into the hole are really the final answer. Nevertheless, a sound style and method of making the stroke builds up a great deal of confidence in one's own ability.

Judgment is something that can only be achieved by experience. By this, I mean that good judgment can only be installed into one's brain by continually practising in a sensible and orderly fashion. Judging the speed of a green is difficult so it is necessary to study the line of the putt as regards to the amount of moisture in the turf, how close the grass has been mown, and what effect the undulations will have on the ball. An orderly study of these and other factors combined with the experience of practice and serious rounds of golf will enhance your judgment and make putting a more enjoyable part of the game.

Working out how much "borrow" to take on a putt, in other words how far to the side of a hole one should hit the ball for it to curl back and drop together with how hard to hit the ball, can only come with experience. It is surprising how many golfers do not learn by their mistakes, also how many players do not have the courage to take the line of putt they know they should. Take the saying: "You missed that one on the amateur's side." This applies to the case where there is a sideways slope. Let us for the moment assume that the green is sloping from left to right so the ball will have to start out to the left of the hole and will curl back to the right. If hit correctly, the ball will drop, if the ball passes the hole on the left side it is "missed on the professional's side": if it misses the right side of the hole it "misses on the amateur's side".

Why are these terms used? There is a greater margin of error on the left side than on the right side of the hole. Professionals have learnt from experience that the ball is more likely to drop into the hole on the left side, so generally speaking they will take a little more "borrow" than will most amateurs. That is why if a putt is missed on the left side it is more likely to be a professional holding the putter. The two factors involved here are: 1. the professional has had more experience because he plays more golf and 2. his experience has taught him to have the courage of his convictions. The amateur, generally speaking, is lacking in both, but there is nothing to stop him having the determination to put into operation the factors he knows to be correct by simply being orderly and sensible about it.

Another common error for the amateur is being short of the hole, in other words, not giving the stroke sufficient power to get the ball as far as the hole. Possibly the most used expression on the putting green is "never up, never in". This expression cannot be over emphasised for the shorter and medium length putts, because you should be expecting to drop a good proportion of them, and nothing is more certain than the fact that a putt that is short will never go in. A good plan when practising is to penalise yourself every time a putt stops short. For instance, you can take the putts in batches of six each time, line up six balls about four or five inches apart and if any of the six fall short you immediately retrieve those you have played and completely discount that batch and consider that you have made no progress from the situation immediately prior to that batch. In other words, that particular batch was a waste of time. Very few people will be content in knowing they are wasting time and most will buck up their ideas by being more and more determined that every batch of six balls will be made to count in the overall progress. Always be determined and perhaps aggressive in your approach to putting practice.

It is well worth mentioning that it is far more important to practice the short putts than the long ones. Being confident of getting the short ones means that one is not so worried about going past the hole when playing a long putt, even well past, therefore you will not often be short and will at least have given the ball a chance. Yet, it is surprising that so few golfers take time out to practise the short ones; they would much rather practise from a distance of 10 feet or more. Take my advice and practise from six feet and under until you become quite proficient and you will find the longer ones improving automatically.

Finally, the way you address the ball and your style of putting should be based on maximum comfort and confidence. With confidence in mind always be ready to alter your style if you are having problems – even in the middle of a game. Above all never be afraid to experiment.

There are still a few well-known playing and teaching professionals who believe that it is possible to apply topspin or overspin to a ball in a putting stroke and they often advise it in order to make the ball "stay on line". Scientists have conclusively shown by experiment and calculation that like normal shots in the air topspin is quite impossible. Any effort spent in trying to achieve overspin is completely wasted. The true facts are as follows: any putting stroke will result in the ball sliding over the putting surface as it leaves the club for the first part of the distance and then the friction between the grass and the ball will stop the sliding action, at which point the ball begins to roll normally. With the ball suitably marked, high speed movie film will prove it to be so.

A ball can only be considered to have topspin when the surface of the ball is sliding in relation to the surface of the green, spinning forwards if you like, and this cannot happen. Not by any stretch of imagination can rolling be considered as overspin. Please understand this – there is no such thing as topspin on the putting green. Any ideas about making the ball "dive" into the hole by imparting topspin are a complete waste of time and sometimes these ideas can be harmful because the player's energies are being concentrated on useless pursuits instead of useful practice. The golf world is full of misconceptions as I have pointed out so often in these pages.

You may have heard the expressions "You sliced that putt" or "You hooked that one". The amount of sidespin that can be imparted during a putting stroke is so small as to have no effect on the direction of travel. This sidespin idea has also been proven to be a fallacy.

If you are a snooker or billiard player, you may find the following very interesting. You will have seen good players swerve the cue ball at speed in order to get out of a snooker. The amount of combined sidespin and backspin required to swerve the ball just a small amount is really quite tremendous and it does not need much imagination to see that it is impossible to apply this sort of spin to a golf ball. The reason for the large difference in amount of spin is in the different way the power is applied to the ball. In the case of the cue, the power is applied through the tip, which is chalked to increase the grip at a point on the ball as far as possible from the ball's centre of gravity and in the direction required. Even in the hands of an expert, the putter could not apply the spin necessary to make the ball curl unless a tip was attached to the top of the handle and it was used like a cue.

All this really means is that sidespin on the putting green is of no consequence whatever and therefore it is just not possible to slice or hook a putt. Now, having disposed of topspin and sidespin let us consider the really important factors and begin by looking at the three essentials of a good putt. For the moment let us assume that the area of the green over which the ball has to travel is perfectly flat, level and in excellent condition. Then the three essentials are:

1)   At the moment of impact the face of the putter must be square to the hole.

2)   The ball must be struck on the sweet spot of the putter.

3)   The putter blade must be swung on line to the hole.

For all golfers who feel there is plenty of room for improvement and, above all, who really do wish to make an improvement, I first of all suggest that a long, hard look at the three essentials is necessary before experimenting with a change of style. One of my pupils had a reasonably good style but was discontented with the fact that he had difficulty in hitting the ball on the right line, for the shorter putts. He had not appreciated that most of his putts were missing the hole on the left side. When questioned, he admitted that about eight or nine out of ten "missed" shots did in fact do this and my first reaction was to examine the squareness of the putter blade at address. When he corrected this, the putts began to drop but whether he put this into practise consistently later on would depend almost entirely on his mental approach.

I am sure it is true to say that the amount of attention given to the three essentials, when practising at home on the carpet or on the course, is not sufficient mainly because their significance is not properly appreciated. Not so many golfers, for instance, fully appreciate that not only does a putt move to the right of the intended line when hit with the toe of the putter, but also it will finish short of a true sweet-spot-contacted putt, because part of the energy has been wasted by the impact turning the blade.

I am aware that some of you will immediately say: "But I have hit putts on the toe of the blade and the shot did not finish right of the line." Yes, I have done this myself and the real reason is that sometimes one instinctively realises that the toe is coming into the ball and at the last moment one compensates by "closing" the blade a little. I am sure the more experienced players will admit to having occasionally produced a "toed" putt that finished left of the hole.

However, it is not a good thing to have to compensate for an error during a swing, whether on the putting green or anywhere else. It is a good thing to try out, if only at home on the carpet, the effects of not complying with the three essentials, in varying combinations. There is no substitute for experience, and experiencing errors on purpose (on a short-term basis) is a quick way of deepening one's understanding of the game, and can help one to avoid the error by simply being aware of it.

It is interesting to try out the following exercises on the carpet, using an ashtray as the hole.

1) Swing the putter blade "on line" to target, leaving the face "open" (say 10° open) and be sure you contact the sweet spot. You will find the ball travelling several degrees to the right of the target, quite sufficient to easily miss the hole. Having done this a few times to verify the consistency of the result, correct the blade alignment to a square position at impact and practise carefully the three essentials.

2) Swing the putter blade on line and attempt to keep the face square at impact, but make contact on the toe of the putter. This exercise is quite difficult because, knowing you are going to "toe" it, you will have a strong tendency to close the blade as you approach impact, in order to compensate. You may be able to overcome this tendency by consciously keeping the back of the left hand facing (at impact) as it was at address. Having done this several times correct the error by contacting the sweet spot and note the different line the ball takes. Also take note that thinking deeply about contacting the ball on the sweet spot appears psychologically to help you to perform a good putt.

3) Swing the putter purposely off line, keeping the blade square to the hole and contact the sweet spot. You will find that the blade has to be swung off line to an amazing degree to miss the target by a big margin. From this you can deduce that the aforementioned third essential – an "on line swing" – is the least important of the three. Never be afraid to try out "errors" on purpose. This is a different thing altogether from continually practising and ironing in unconscious errors. When you occasionally try out an error to prove a theory, you are deepening your understanding. It is a good route to permanent improvement, and anyway it makes life more interesting.

GOLF: THE TRUTH

POSTSCRIPT

It's all in the mind

You know now the dynamics of the golf swing: you know why the ball bursts off to the right and the left: you know how to hit the ball straight down the middle, the one shot which is sought by golfers in their thousands; and you know the truth of it all. But, to be perfectly frank, that is not quite all that is required to be a player of substance and merit. The other factor in this tantalising game is deep in the mind; in the mind of the individual who holds the club in his hands and upon his mental approach is built the winning game. And, here again, I can help.

As I was finishing off this book I watched on the television screen the splendid 1985 Open Championship win by Britain's Sandy Lyle at Sandwich on the coast in Kent. Britain had waited 16 years for another home-bred champion to follow Tony Jacklin, but I am sorry to say that Lyle is not a player who, I feel, will go on to put his stamp on the golf world as such men before him as Palmer, Nicklaus, Trevino, and Ballesteros have done since they took the British title. To put it bluntly, Sandy Lyle, so far in his career, is not the fighter or mental player of the calibre of those great champions. He plays golf without mental conviction, as do 99% of players – and that means you.

As I watched Lyle being presented with the Open trophy, my thoughts took me ahead in time, "What about the future?". I wished I could get hold of Lyle for just six months. All those who are close to him must recognise that he could do with that extra pinch of determination that is possessed by Bernhard Langer. The German's attempt to sink his final iron shot at the 18th from just off the green was a joy to behold. No holding back, he went for it tooth and nail. He wasn't content to opt for second place, a true example of his attitude of mind. He's got that essential ingredient needed to win consistently which was developed in his early days on the tournament circuit when being a fighter was essential for survival.

Lyle needs this killer instinct in his competitive make-up. But, how on earth does he, or you for that matter, acquire it? In the first place you must start talking to yourself, putting thoughts of success into the mind. Call it self-hypnosis. Use the power of positive thought and enjoy the experience. Don't make it hard work. But, how the hell, you may ask, do you do this in golf?

I have found one thought process particularly helpful and it is this. Use the ball itself as your only focal point for your swing thoughts. As you approach the ball, whatever the shot to be played, keep repeating forcefully to yourself, "I am going to SWING through that ball with ease and grace (*using no more than 80% full power*) and freewheel through it." Try it.

I would dearly love Lyle to give it a determined trial. I would also like to see Lyle practising to achieve the "straight shot" as his standard stock-in-trade shot which can come with the freewheeling concept. Freewheeling is exactly what should be happening when the wrists and hands are under the control of centrifugal force. The bad shots arrive mostly because the right hand works much too hard, trying to do the work which centrifugal force does so easily. Try to use CF; don't destroy it.

Before a shot is played there are decisions to

42: A dismayed Sandy Lyle watches his fluffed chip shot to the 18th green in the last round of the 1985 British Open: 'He plays golf without mental conviction, as do 99% of players.'

be made such as which club to use and whether to punch the ball into the wind or float it high. Once these problems are settled you are back to making the shot and this is where Lyle, like a great many professionals, does not take enough care. When it comes to setting themselves up most professionals line-up the clubface to the target, not realising that it is extremely difficult to square up a three-inch long blade to a target 200 yards away. Then they compound the error by carelessly lining the feet square to the clubface. Simple geometry tells me that my method is a much sounder proposition.

Do it this way: line up the feet first by turning the head, not tilting it, use the eyes to strike an imaginary but accurate line across the toes to the target. Then square-up the clubface to the toe line. You are now firing directly at the target. Lyle, together with his colleagues, may well think that I am talking through my hat but, believe me, I have not carried out 17 years of intensive study to be wrong on such a basic point.

Finally, Sandy Lyle's backswing, as everyone can see, is more strongly inside the down-swing than most other professionals. To bring a marked improvement to his already good shot-making, I would like him to try to get his backswing nearer to the downswing path in order to reduce his in-to-out loop during the backswing to downswing transition. I would ask him to make it a habit-forming procedure and in no way should he allow this backswing correction to dominate his thoughts during competitive play.

To win again and then again, Sandy Lyle must tighten-up his mental approach and for us lesser mortals, the same must apply. It is all very well knowing the truth about the golf swing as I have set it out here but it is another thing to make the most of it out on the course. So now, get determined and become a winner.

And finally . . .

After all has been said, statements of fact, revelations of the truth, thoughts, feelings and opinions, there remains that elusive element of life-luck. Some people call it fortune. We must accept that somewhere down the line it will play its part, whether a major or a minor one, but it is undoubtedly true that to some extent one can make one's own luck by using a positive approach.

By the time some of you have read this book Sandy Lyle may have won more than another title or two and taken some confidence from his part in Europe's Ryder Cup victory over the United States. He may have had some good luck; he may have read this book and taken it seriously – who knows?

What is most important is that the amateurs, the club golfers of the world, who keep this game so alive should be given the best possible chance to improve their game and thus their enjoyment of it.

THIS IS WHAT THIS BOOK IS REALLY ALL ABOUT!

CREDITS